TRAVELLING LIGHT

Daniel J. O'Leary

Travelling Light

YOUR JOURNEY TO WHOLENESS

A book of 'Breathers' to inspire you along the way

the columba press

First published in 2001 by
the columba press
55A Spruce Avenue, Stillorgan Industrial Park, Blackrock, Co Dublin

Reprinted 2003, 2004

Cover by Bill Bolger
Origination by The Columba Press
Printed in Ireland by Colour Books Ltd, Dublin

ISBN 1 85607 319 X

Acknowledgements
The author and publisher gratefully acknowledge the permission of the
following to use material in their copyright: Tarcher/Putnam, New
York for *Living Presence* by Kabir Edmund Helminski; Ave Maria Press,
Notre Dame, Indiana for *May I have this dance?* by Joyce Rupp; The
Acorn Press for *I am that* by Nisargadatta Maharay; Faber and Faber Ltd
for *Via Negativa* by R. S. Thomas; Orbis Books, Maryknoll, NY for
'Christianity and Creation' by Richard Rohr; Darton, Longman and
Todd Ltd for *Sharing the Darkness* by Sheila Cassidy (1988); Macmillan
General Books for poems by Tagore; Element Books for *Divine Light and
Fire* by Peter de Coppens; The Editor of *Spirituality* for two quotations
from an article by Joan Chittister; The Editor of *The Furrow* for a quot-
ation from an article by Sebastian Moore; Grove/Atlantic Inc. for *Dream
Work* by Mary Oliver; Harper San Francisco for *The Tibetan Book of
Living and Dying* by Sogyal Rinpoche; John Bate for *Damaged Beauty
needs a New Design*; Daniel Ladinsky for poems from *I Heard God
Laughing: Renderings of Hafiz*, copyright 1996.
Every effort has been made to trace copyright holders. If we have inadvertently used copyright material without permission we apologise
and will put it right in future editions.

Contents

Dedication and Acknowledgements   9

Introduction   11

PART ONE: PACK NOTHING

A reflection before setting out   14

PART TWO: THIRTY-ONE BREATHERS FOR THE JOURNEY

Day 1   Listen to your body   28

Day 2   Mind your mind   32

Day 3   Know your ego   36

Day 4   Grow by subtraction   41

Day 5   Take the second take   44

Day 6   Notice the grace of space   47

Day 7   Dance the dance   51

Day 8   Paint on a broader canvas   55

Day 9   Meet God halfway   60

Day 10   Where is your bright face?   65

Day 11   Be a living sacrifice of praise   69

Day 12   Have you the courage to be?   73

Day 13   Lighten up   76

Day 14   Can you let go of fear?   80

Day 15   Do you know how loved you are?   84

Day 16   Look out! Beyond here be dragons   88

Day 17   Transform the negative cycle   92

Day 18   Trust that all is harvest   97

Day 19   Create a bit of heaven on earth   101

Day 20   Send for reinforcements   106

Day 21   Become what you love   110

Day 22   Know your heart-power   114

Day 23   Celebrate your age   118

Day 24   Listen to your inner child   123

Day 25   Be a child of the universe   127

Day 26   Unblock, release, connect   133

Day 27   Don't miss the moment   139

Day 28   Be an alchemist   144

Day 29   Embrace your shadow   148

Day 30   Live in the present   153

Day 31   Travelling light   157

Nota Bene: You are called to be authentic, not perfect   172

PART THREE: AT A NEW THRESHOLD

High Noon at Ghost Ranch:
          A message from the desert   176

Riding the Santa Fe bus:
          A theological note on 'simply being'   186

Dawn over Lebh Shomea :
          Pray as you can, not as you should   196

Glossary   212

Notes   214

Provide yourselves with no gold or silver,
not even with a few coppers for your purses;
with no haversack for the journey
or spare tunic or footwear or a staff. . .
(Mt 10:9-10)

Thus God says to these bones:
'I will cause breath to enter you,
and you shall live.'
(Ezek 37:5)

Tom, aged four, very early one morning, rushed
into the bedroom exclaiming in great excitement,
'Marg, I can breathe! I can breathe! Watch me! Watch me!'
Deep noisy breaths, in and out, then,
'Can *you* breathe?'
'Yes.'
'Show me! Show me!'
(Margaret Siberry in *Passion for the Possible*)

The present moment is where life can be found, and if you don't arrive
there, you miss your appointment with life. You don't have to run anymore. Breathing in, we say, 'I have arrived.' Breathing out, we say, 'I
am home.' This is a very strong practice, a very deep practice.
(Thich Nhat Hahn in *The Present Moment*)

Throw away
All your begging bowls at God's door;

For I have heard the Beloved
prefers sweet threatening shouts,

Something in the order of:

'Hey, Beloved,
My heart is a raging volcano
Of love for you!

You better start kissing me –
Or Else!'

(Hafiz in *I Heard God Laughing*)

7

Dedication and Acknowledgements

I dedicate *Travelling Light* to all those who befriended and encouraged me during my recent sabbatical time. The first weeks were spent with the Carmelite Sisters at Thicket Priory near Selby in Yorkshire. They always welcome me with warmth. Father Abbot and the community of Benedictine monks at Pluscarden, near Inverness in Scotland, were my gracious hosts for many more weeks. I joined Sr Pat, the staff and participants at The Franciscan Spiritual Centre in Minnesota, during the late winter and early spring of 2000. It was there, by the banks of the Mississippi, that I learned to cross-country ski and wrote most of this book. Almost everyone at the Centre read and commented on the manuscript. They will recognise their words of wisdom throughout these pages.

After that I stayed at Madonna House in the Santa Fe Archdiocesan Headquarters in Albuquerque where Dominic, John and Luis looked after me. By a window with a stunning view of the Rio Grande valley, it was easy to meditate. While there I visited the Centre for Action and Contemplation founded and directed by the Franciscan priest Richard Rohr and shared in an unforgettable men's retreat with him. I continued with my reflecting and writing in a lovely summer-house on the Galveston coast in Southern Texas, as guest of Sr Kathleen Daly and the Sisters of Charity (Houston) of the Incarnate Word.

From there I travelled to Lebh Shomea House of Prayer in Sarita, between Corpus Christi and the Mexican border, for a 40-day desert retreat. This 'school of solitary prayer' exists under the auspices of the Missionary Oblates of Mary Immaculate. I was there at the time of the 'triple-digit' heat wave across the southern States. These temperatures, combined with the fairly strict silence, and my encounters with a few of my favourite demons, made this a most memorable experience! Fr Kelly Nemeck OMI, two hermits – Sr Marie Theresa Coombs and Sr Maria Meister – and the delightful Fr Patrick took great care of us and provided nourishment for body and soul. I ended the sabbatical with a chance to review my adventures and pull them

all together in these pages, with the ever-loving help of Sr
Kathleen Dalton and as a spoiled guest of the Sisters of Charity
(Halifax) in Nova Scotia, Canada.

I hope that Sean Fagan SM, Margaret Siberry, Linda Marsh,
Gill Davis and Fr Mark Noonan CM will be touched by
Travelling Light. They suggested, as I set out on my recent quest,
that I should make some notes. Together with my bishop, David
Konstant, they have a trust in my writing abilities, especially
when I'm full of doubt. The belief that Seán O Boyle of Columba
Press would give this book a warm welcome, provided me with
a great incentive to complete the task when motivation ran low.
To him and Brian and all at Columba, I wish God speed on their
own journeys.

These are some of the people who breathed and walked with
me on my spiritual journey. Their invisible faces and forms flit
in and out of the pages as you turn them over. Their open and
honest hands and hearts were the securest of places for me to do
the work I had to do, to write the book I had to write, to shed the
tears I had to shed. Wherever they are, may they grace the earth,
and walk beautifully upon it.

I also dedicate this book to those special people who, over the
years, have encouraged me, trusted me, believed in me, loved
me and held me safe. In spite of (or maybe because of!) my 'sins',
they never gave up on me. Nor have they ever diminished me.
They have only magnified my soul. These angels are, for me, the
intimate faces of God. They are my teachers, and the energy of
my life. I now know they will never be far away. And the
ground between us will always be holy ground.

Introduction

Are you at some kind of crossroads in your life? Do you feel weighed down with unnecessary baggage? Do you have a sense that there should be more to life than what you are now experiencing? Take heart. There are millions like you. And very many of them are finding a new joy and freedom in their daily living once they nourish the needs of the 'hidden self'. Even though the decades are flying by and we do not get another chance of living the abundant life, there is still time. So for God's sake and your own, begin.

There are two questions to ask yourself. Do you feel a call to deepen your life, to live more freely, to be more happy? And the second is, are you prepared to take the time and the trouble to discover this new way of living, and to enjoy it forever? The aim of this book is to empower you to respond 'Yes' to both questions and to travel along the amazing way with you.

It takes courage and trust to take the first step. There will be voices within and without telling you to wait, or that you haven't got what it takes, or to forget it. But if you are ready, and since you are reading this you must be, the way is already being cleared for you.

There is a yearning within all of us to be leaner, looser and lighter in body and soul. We long to be healed of, detached from resentment, grief, fear, jealousy, anger and low self-esteem. The wings and roots of our hearts are coded for free flight and for the grounded love and service of each other.

I have just completed a year's sabbatical devoted entirely to nourishing the spiritual dimension of my life. Written from the heart of this journey, *Travelling Light* is designed to be a companion for you, too, as you decide to set out on your own inner adventures. Part One offers reflections before setting out and prepares us for the pattern of our journeying. The starting point is that deep longing within each of us for 'the pearl of great price', and once felt, it will not go away. The reflections guide us through those first, scary and tentative movements into the unknown, when we feel the pain of letting go of so much that seems to be the foundation of our security and comfort.

The *Breathers* (Part Two), at the heart of the book, are short meditations and practices for those who set out on this path of their bliss. The adventures will be many. The road unsure. The pain never far away. These daily *Breathers* are written from within the conflicts of my own soul. They sustain me and fill me with courage each new day. I hope they will do the same for you. What is essential is to keep trusting and letting go, to stay open and vulnerable, to live only in the present moment.

The challenge of the spiritual life is not to make more and longer pilgrimages, to say more and longer prayers. It is to explore more deeply into what we already are so that we will live, like second nature, the good news which we already possess. In order to travel light along the path of our inner journey, we do not have to devour more and more books; we only have to continually reflect on the few lines of truth that nourish the heart, and to put that piece of wisdom into practice. In our deepest self, it is to become by habit what we know by heart. One lived sentence can change a life. 'Even a thought, even a possibility,' wrote Friedrich Nietzsche, 'can shatter us and transform us.' And, once our true mind is stretched by a new idea or vision, it never regains its original shape! May God speed you on your journey.

Part Three, the final part of the book, contains three longer meditations that emerged from my graced travelling with different companions and in different settings during my sabbatical year. Written out of a theology of creation and a spirituality of the heart, they draw together many of the insights I gained along the way but they reveal an essential truth – that once reached, the horizon shifts again, and that the journey itself is all. That is why I encourage readers to repeat the daily reflections and practices month after month, for I know, everyday, the vital part they play in my own journey towards becoming an authentic human being.

PART ONE

Pack Nothing

Rake the muck this way. Rake the muck that way.
It will still be muck. In the time you are brooding,
you could be on your way, stringing pearls
for the delight of heaven.
(Hasidic teaching)

A reflection before setting out

AT SOME STAGE in our lives, most of us will set out on some kind of spiritual quest. 'And tell me,' the poet asks, 'what will you do with your one, wild and precious life?' It may be as a last resort when things go very wrong, it may be due to the influence of a friend, it may be when nothing else seems to satisfy our deeper needs. This book is about pacing yourself during that inner journey; about stopping to breathe along the way; about inspirational milestones so as to keep your bearings when there are lots of false signals around you. There will be many times when we need to centre ourselves by breathing in deeply, by nourishing our hearts with new images, affirmations and reassurances. Without such oases in which to catch our breath, check our maps, nourish our souls, we are liable to wander off in all directions.

The Tyranny of Uprooting
It is not always easy to hear the call to move inwards to the centre of our being, in search of the pearl of great price. This quiet call may also challenge and critique, as it did with me, our normal routine of work and style of life, even in radical ways. When we do finally recognise that persistent voice, there is a great temptation to ignore it. We are anxious about what we may have to leave behind and what might happen to us along the way. Most of us fear the unknown. I certainly did a year ago, when I first became aware of the deep intimations that would not go away. The stirrings I was feeling were not about 'time out' for further study or sabbatical travel, but about a need to explore the mystery of my own being.

When I first began to listen to that vague prompting inside me, a thousand reasons for ignoring it rushed in. Our beautiful new church had just been built and dedicated; I felt supported and affirmed in my ministry by faithful and trusting parishioners; also, the next few years in our new presbytery could only be less frenetic and more peaceful. Even though at 63 I was getting on a bit, I was still in good health and looking forward to working with our prayerful, collaborative community which was vibrant with creative and compassionate ministries of service. Why then did I not listen to reason? Well out of range of the mid-life crisis, why did I feel the call to do this foolish thing? Was I being utterly naïve to imagine I could survive without the friendships, comforts and work that I enjoyed so much? Had I the courage to let go of all of this, and feel the insecurity of loss, the anxiety about the unknown, the fear of being called a fool?

Yet there was no going back. I knew, somehow, that the voice within was authentic. It belonged to that place of truth within us, which, if we can reach it, will never betray us. It is the safest place from which to make a radical decision or simply to reflect on our life – past, present, and future. So often, when our fragile grasp on existence becomes damaged, or when we're torn between options about the best way forward, or when weighing up the pros and cons of arguments and serious decisions, we need a well-nourished heart for the clearest indication of the truest horizon. Once we find our way to that soul-space where God lives, once we negotiate the shadow-lands that surround our inner, holy light, then the maps we draw, the paths we follow, the significant changes we make in our careers and relationships – all such external efforts and outward activities will carry a gracious authenticity and a convincing power because they have grown from our inner silence; they will be sealed by the authority of God.

The *Breathers* and reflections were put together at the beginning of this new century, during my own sabbatical journey at The Spiritual Centre in North America. I felt the need for a ready-to-hand summary of the thoughts and images that I find most helpful for keeping, from day to day, a spiritual and psychological health and balance. I call upon them to create a welcome relief, a spiritual focus to ground myself when suddenly surrounded by negative thoughts or oppressive people. For many travellers on the path of their bliss, the evening or at night is the best time to pray. For me, the morning is the only time I can free my mind and heart and body to meditate and focus on the image or *Breather* that seems appropriate. And yet, how often have I forced the promptings of the Holy Spirit from my heart, as I compulsively rushed to my early desk to finish yesterday's left-over work, so as to be ready for another frantic day. On such occasions I have rarely found the time to pray later. In

his lovely book *Sabbath*, Wayne Muller quotes an old Hasidic
poem:

> Take special care to guard your
> tongue before the morning prayer.
> Even greeting your fellow, we are told,
> can be harmful at that hour.
> A person who wakes up in the morning is
> like a new creation.
> If you begin your day with unkind words,
> or even trivial matters –
> even though you may later turn to prayer,
> you have not been true to your Creation.
> All of your words each day
> are related to one another.
> All of them are rooted
> in the first words that you speak.

A most important dimension to the *Breathers* is that they are set
against my current experiences here at the Centre, with its em-
phasis on the necessity for body-work and breathing techniques,
since body, mind and spirit are always inseparable on the spiritual path. There is something very significant about this revelation. Let me try to explain it a little.

Love's Thinking Body
My head and heart are full of ideas and images about spirituality,
wholeness and holiness. After all, I have spent decades learning
and writing about the Four Paths of Creation Spirituality, about
the gifts and shadows that merge and mix within us, as we journey home towards ourselves, others and therefore God, about
personal reflections on a theology of creation and numerous
related psychological, spiritual and pedagogical dimensions of
our response to the call of Jesus to the abundant life. What needs
much more attention now, I believe, is the way in which we incorporate, 'flesh out', so to speak, our knowledge and wisdom
into the texture and reality of our body/mind wholeness. To
have insightful, doctrinal notions about being 'in the state of
grace' about 'doing God's will' and about 'travelling the spiritual
path' is one thing, but to actually experience these realities in
our bodies, as an awareness of aliveness and energy, of ease and
grace, is quite another. We need to understand more profoundly

why our bodies are called 'temples of the Holy Spirit'; why they have a role in awakening us to, and in expressing our spirituality; why they are shrines and tabernacles of the indwelling Trinity; why, according to Tertullian, 'it is on the flesh that the hinge of salvation turns'.

On the one hand, the Catholic tradition of Christianity is wonderfully earthy, sacramental and physical, with its insistence on natural, archetypal elements as the symbols for worship, its uses of ashes, water, incense, oil and wax in its sacramentals and paraliturgies, its rustic and robust celebration of Ember and Rogation Days, its old rituals of prayer to the four directions, in time and tune with the seasons of the year, its relentless adherence to the reality of the Body and Blood of Jesus at Mass, its worship of the totally human body of the Risen Christ in heaven. How strange then that, in spite of this rich and resonant tradition, so much of our theology, scripture work, worship and praying is almost entirely located in the head. The dualistic fear of the body is still such a controlling power in our understanding of the mystery of the incarnation and in our living-out of our Christian baptism and eucharist.

The mystics had no such hang-ups. For them our bodies are the skins of the spirit, our souls made touchable, the time and space expression of the Pure Being of Love. They realised that spiritual visions and devotions were of little real use until they were embodied and grounded in a practical way. Their exceptional and rounded balance of expression and description of centred holiness, their freedom in the use of sensuous images and physical feelings regarding union with God, all combine to delight us with a sense of embodied wisdom, love and power. They knew that we only become whole and radically holy when we learn to integrate our spiritual, transcendent self with our personal, human and fleshly self. The source of their wisdom, the role-model they aspired to was, of course, none other than the manner and truth of the birth of God into our human condition. Bringing about this integration is the function and goal of the journey of healing and wholeness and the main reason for writing this book.

In the incarnation, God achieved that total enfleshing of Love in assuming the full humanity of the baby Jesus. Every cell, muscle, bone, fibre and drop of blood of the human body of the divine boy and adult, were the tangible and visible essence of

God. To be touched by Jesus was to be touched by God. To hear
and see him was to hear and see God. To be hugged and kissed
by Jesus was to be hugged and kissed by God. To smell his
breath was to smell the breath of God. Jesus lived fully in his
body; his physical self was the embodiment of the inner wisdom
he carried in his heart; the way he walked, talked, smiled and
joked were sacramentals of the truest nature of God. When he
ate or fasted and saw to his more mundane bodily functions, he
was shaping the physical contours of the holy Word existing
from the beginning. When he loved his special friends in the
most human of ways and yearned, as we all do, for intimacy,
when he was tempted at every turn, like we all are, and distracted
too, when he was cold or passionate depending on the state of
his self-awareness, his health, the weather, his age – as baby, as
child, as boy, as teenager, as adult – he was completely the presence on earth of his Father in heaven.

In spite of all of this most attractive theology of creation, and
for many well-documented, but hopelessly misguided reasons,
the body has consistently been regarded with suspicion in the
mainstream Christian churches and in most of the spiritual traditions of the West. Against this legacy of dismissing, denying or
ignoring the sacrament of the body, it is extremely difficult for
those with an intuitive or received sense of God, or Being, to embody their beliefs fully, to integrate them into the raw material
of the life of the senses. The challenge is to come down from the
rarified atmosphere of the mountain of visions into the blood,
sweat and tears of messy, daily struggle in the valley of tears.
And that is where power and passion, the inexhaustible wells of
energy, are located and flowing over.

To come from our heads to our hearts, in the first place, and
then from our hearts to our bodies, requires a degree of vulnerability, a willingness to be open to suffering. To be vulnerable is
to risk coming out of our ego-castles where we can settle everything mentally, where we can justify, rationalise and defend our
lifestyle and our prayer-life and our role plays. To be vulnerable
is to fully inhabit our bodies, to live our feelings and emotions,
to own our dark side, to let go of the sham and pretence etched
into our way of life for a very long time, to acknowledge our dependence on status, power, money, privilege and relationships.
To be vulnerable is to become authentic and to tell the truth
about our real motives, our fears and terrors. To bring our spirit-

uality into our bodies, into our lived experiences, is to be very
vulnerable indeed. It is also to become free.

How does freedom come in? What do we mean by a free person? We mean someone who is not copying someone else, as
so many people have to do to keep their jobs. But what does
it 'mean' to find my motivation 'within'? To most people this
is a mystery. It is only when I have learned – or rather am
learning – to take a few deep breaths, befriend the way I feel
just at this moment, however messed up, and allow my feeling to speak and surprise me so that I breathe a sigh of relief,
it is only then that I begin to know what it is that we are referring to when we speak of acting 'from within'. And when we
catch on to this, freedom becomes a quality, an experience of
self, a state of mind, like joy and peace; and this is the freedom that (truly self-) controls. I know a few free people.[1]

The key to complementing an intellectual understanding of
our faith is to develop a new awareness of our bodies. To truly
live in our bodies is to have a conscious and highly attuned
sense of ourselves as living, moving, breathing, feeling organ-
isms. Take breathing, for example. Is it not extraordinary that the
most vital element in our lives, the one that plays such a central
role in our transformation, is nearly always taken for granted? If
we become aware of the power of our breath, we have the ability
to bring about real change, both psychologically and spiritually.
It is written large into our Story. It all began when God breathed
life into mud. A Sufi mystic wrote, 'All is contained in the Divine
Breath, like the day in the morning's dawn.' In *Breathing Alive*
Reshad Field writes, 'We come into this world on the Breath of
His Compassion, and we go out of this world on the Breath of
His Mercy.' In between these two eternal Breaths, all creation,
human and other-than-human, share in this most wondrous
'moment' with our little breaths of air, the only element on
Planet Earth that we all have so intimately in common.
Attention to our breathing will be referred to in each day's
Breather.

Breather One and *Breather Two* set the scene for this understanding of holistic growing and spiritual mindfulness – an
understanding that permeates all the *Breathers*. Many practical
suggestions regarding the achievement of such an integration of
our spiritual selves are made throughout the book. And when
we seek to *become* this transformed consciousness that leads to

an integrated sense of the whole of our being, it is something more than a mere understanding or knowledge of the miracle of our lives. It is more than a deeper grasp and perception of the marvels of our body, mind and spirit entities. It springs from, and is nourished by a spirit of awe, like the overwhelmed heart of the psalmist who wrote, 'It was you who created my inmost self, and put me together in my mother's womb. For all these mysteries I thank you. For the wonder of myself . . .' (Ps 139).

The False Self

The reason for having to set out on the journey, in the first place, is because of what we call the ego, or the false self. The whole thrust of each of the *Breathers* is to grapple with the tyranny of the ego. (*Breather Three* briefly explores the almost unbelievable, hidden influence exerted over us by the awesome power of ego-ism.) When we are trying to transcend our negative emotions – the resentment, the cynicism, the fear, the jealousy, the low self-esteem, with which most of us are quite familiar – what we are seeking is our true heart, our true self, because, to some extent, we are all slaves of our false self. At some time in our childhood, or maybe a little later, we began to live an adapted, conditioned life of pretence.

It began, simply, as our way of coping with the imperfection of our parents, our schooling and with the belief systems we in-herited, that imposed on us a huge amount of guilt, fear and shame. The resulting amalgam of acquired prejudices, taboos, and anxieties that often leads to neuroses and psychological imbalance, must be explored, exposed and understood, if the spiritual journey is ever to get underway. In spite of all the sur-vival strategies that become so costly in later life, in terms of meaninglessness, depression and emptiness, there is a true self that is very damaged, but not dead, deep within us.

How do we transcend and transform the ego? How do we breathe life again into our lost, true self? Can we even identify the ego, so clever and plausible are its persuasions, so totally in control has it grown within us? Most of the wise and holy people agree, that if we are to reach an appropriate maturity and re-sponsible individuality, we must discern our egotism from our true self, and we begin to do this by keeping a vigilant watch over the arrogance and self-righteousness of the ego. The ego is not all bad. It is shaped through our efforts to cope, survive and manoeuvre for a place from which to hold our own. It is fundamentally a positive, organising energy whose source is the Spirit and whose function is to be a reliable servant, messenger and friend. We need to tame the tyrant-ego and to nurture the co-creator-ego. This is a long journey. But the wind is at our back.

So much of this book is about awareness and living in the present moment. This loving but objective observing, in the here and now, is the first (and probably the last) step to be taken in the journey towards spiritual freedom and light.

By keeping the mirror of awareness clear, we can begin to free ourselves of our compulsions and inappropriate thoughts and behaviour. Awareness is the means; the present moment is the focus. We have certain obstacles to face. We must confront our lack of attention and weakness of will, our attachment to our opinions, our slavery to our likes and dislikes, and our perpetual fear of loss. All of these characteristics form the main material for the work of transformation, to be transformed by the resonance of love, the power of our essential self. It is necessary to awaken to this self, which has the power of love that can tame the false self, the ego . . . If we could just be, we would be able to relax from the anxiety of becoming something that we are not, getting something we don't have, and trying to shape reality according to our own desires. And yet what we most need is what we already are – our essential self. There is no escape; there is only coming home.[2]

The Journey Home

What is important about the journey home is that we begin it. That beginning calls for courage. And staying with it calls for courage too. It is God who does the transforming; all we have to do is show up and start walking. Silently, invisibly, we are purified. As we walk we become lighter, leaner, looser. We see things more clearly as we gradually become more empty. And the emptier we become, the more room there is for God to fill us. The more fine-tuned we are, the sweeter will sound the tunes of God. The more hollow we are, the truer the music from the lips of the Flautist. Joyce Rupp captures this image so beautifully.

A small, wooden flute,
an empty, hollow reed,
rests in her silent hand.

It awaits the breath
of one who creates song
through its open form.

My often-empty life
rests in the hand of God;
like the hollowed flute,
it yearns for the melody
which only Breath can give.

The small wooden flute and I,
we need the one who breathes,
we await one who makes melody.

And the one whose touch creates,
awaits our empty, ordinary forms,
so that the song-starved world
may be fed with golden melodies.[3]

These *Breathers* are all written from within my own soul's journey. In fact I began the venture for my own personal benefit,
before deciding to publish the finished work. Some of them
have 'saved' me many a time and have provided me also with a
way to a deeper meditation when the moment of panic or desperation has passed. They are like the familiar friends, all inter-
connected, that we call and rely on to see us through the moments
of distress, self-doubt or beautiful breakthroughs into higher,
brighter places; like wise *anam-chara*s that never fail to enrich
and empower us at the ordinary and extraordinary moments of
our precious lives. And, regarding the breakthrough into enlightenment, I now believe that, if we do differentiate between
people, the difference lies, not in the fact that some people have
negative emotions and other, more spiritual people, do not.
What matters is that, while all, by virtue of their humanity, experience daily temptations, trials and negative feelings, some,
like Jesus, manage to transcend them fairly quickly, while others,
victims of their own and others' egos, stay hopelessly stuck for
far too long in their closed, self-destructive cycle.

I'm aware that the *Breathers* in this book, (apart from
Breathers One and Two which form a basic backdrop to the
whole journey) are shaped only to fit short moments of respite to
carry us through the day, until there's time for more substantial

rest, prayer, reading or talking with a friend. It is quite surprising how deep, complete and effective even a fleeting visit to the sanctuary of our souls can be. Just as many hard-working people have perfected the habit of regaining their energy through strategically-placed ten-minute cat-naps throughout the day, so too, with confident practice, all of us can be empowered by these silent withdrawals into that place within ourselves, that is full of the richest resources of grace and spiritual energy and wisdom. As water is to the fish and sky to the eagle, these moments are pure delight to the soul.

Travelling Light offers thirty one meditations *(Breathers)*, one for every day of the month. They are like different glimpses of the same splendid pearl, circling explorations of God's incarnation, varying angles on one eternal truth. Because each meditation has many layers of meanings – enough spiritual energy for the journey of a lifetime – they can be read anew each month, hopefully at deeper levels of understanding. They need to be pored over, reflected upon, wondered at, rather than merely glanced-at or speed-read. As with mystery, their full significance will never be exhausted – they are like a month of Sundays. A blank space follows each day's *Reflection* and *Praxis* for the reader's own thoughts, experiences, stories, poems or dream accounts. Once the inner journey is embarked upon, it is not uncommon for the traveller to remember dreams more vividly than usual. Honouring and interacting with these dreams is of the greatest importance.

I use the term *Breathers* throughout *Travelling Light* because of what I have learned about the importance, for our all-round well-being, of good breathing and of the attention we pay to it. I hope the reader will catch some of this enthusiasm. Our breathing holds the key to the quality of our inner lives. It is the only bodily function that readily bridges the conscious and subconscious, the physical and the spiritual aspects of ourselves. From his conversation with his grandma (p. 7), no one had to remind Tom that his breath was one of the innumerable gifts and pleasures that we all have available to us at every moment to which we are present.

The context of the creation of an inspirational book is of the greatest importance. As well as being supported by your travelling companions, you need to be closely held by those who love you. It has been my good fortune to be a guest at the Franciscan

Sisters' Spiritual Centre while writing these reflections. Also, the physical environment can make all the difference. Little Falls, in north Minnesota, is the home of Charles A. Lindbergh Jr, the hero of the first trans-Atlantic solo flight in 1927. On most days of last winter and spring I walked through Lindbergh's farm and across the ingenious bridges he built over Pike Creek just before it meanders into the Mississippi River. He needed the bridges to reach and feed the sheep, while his father was (very unsuccessfully!) trying to become governor of the State. And as he walked he dreamed of flying.

As a teenager, the handsome Lindbergh dropped his studies and devoted his energies to fast motorbikes and lying on his back under the stars. 'I want to ride the winds,' he said, ' and be part of the sky.' Skilled with his hands, he invented many useful domestic contraptions. He worked with engines and had high hopes of soaring above the clouds. He flew for short distances. 'The Flying Fool' they called him. One rainy evening, barely clearing the trees at the end of the makeshift runaway in a wet winter's field, he took off into the black mists, on his journey of destiny. A day later, the lone eagle landed in the fields of France. The world erupted. 'The Flying Fool' had become the 'Lord of the Skies', the 'Hero of the World'. Soon after that, however, his own intense, inner quest began. My mother, who lived in the States at that time, often told us the story. His spirit was stretched to the limits through the extremes of love and loss, of fame and shame, of tragedy and death.

Around here, too, a prehistoric Indian group had lived since 1000BC, and in more recent times, the Dakota tribe used the Mississippi as a primary transportation route and camped all along its west banks. This was the blessed and hallowed ground on which I walked and reflected and crafted this book. I felt so lucky and so graced to be surrounded by an atmosphere of such noble and wise traditions on the one hand, and, on the other, by Lindbergh's spirit of daring, imagination and trust as he took to the skies in a way never before attempted. May a little of his in-spiration, aspiration and recklessness of heart, as he set out on a lonely and fearful journey, find its way into our reflections, and from there into your own pilgrim souls.

As well as springing from this rich context, each *Breather* is also underpinned by a theology of creation and a spirituality of the heart. (I have explored some of these themes in my recent book *Passion for the Possible*.) Only glimpses are offered here. My dearest hope is that readers will be healed and inspired (from *spiro*, to breathe) by praying these Spirit-filled *Breathers*, knowing (with St Augustine) that the journey into the self is the journey home to God. We meet and celebrate both together. There are two questions to ask yourself. 'Do you feel you are called forth on a special journey by God?' If the answer is 'yes', then 'Have you the courage and trust to begin?' In *The Journey*, Mary Oliver wrote:

> One day you finally knew
> what you had to do, and began,
> though the voices around you
> kept shouting
> their bad advice –
> though the whole house
> began to tremble
> and you felt the old tug
> at your ankles .
> … … … … …
> It was already late
> enough, and a wild night,
> and the road full of fallen
> branches and stones.
> But little by little,
> as you left their voices behind,
> the stars began to burn
> through the sheets of clouds,
> and there was a new voice,
> which you slowly
> recognised as your own,
> that kept you company
> as you strode deeper and deeper
> into the world,
> determined to do
> the only thing you could do –
> determined to save
> the only life you could save.[4]

PART TWO

Thirty-One Breathers for the Journey

Traveller, your footprints are
the only path, the only track:
wayfarer, there is no way,
there is no map or Northern star,
just a blank page and a starless dark,
and should you turn round to admire
the distance that you've made today,
the road will billow into dust.
No way on and no way back,
there is no way, my comrade: trust
your own quick step, the end's delay,
the vanished trail of your own wake,
wayfarer, sea-walker, Christ.
(Don Paterson)

Listen to your body

DAY 1

Have you heard of 'body wisdom'? Did you know that your body is the wisest part of you; that it can only tell the truth and that it remembers every-thing? Did you know that every experience you've ever had is stored up in your body, and that your every thought and feeling affects every cell and nerve ending in it? While, like you, I have probably known all of this, and have written and talked about the interconnectedness of mind, body and spirit at great length, what I was still lacking was the *process* and experience of *becoming* what I knew, of *realising* my wisdom, of *doing* my theory. I can only speak for myself, of course, and as a man (because women, in general, are more in touch with their bodies than we are) but I now realise that having information and knowledge stored up in my head, about even the holiest of things, is but a small part of full awareness and true wisdom.

Why do I place this theme at the very beginning of our spirit-ual journey? Because I have come to realise that the body is the forgotten and ignored dimension of wholeness and holiness. Having written several books on the theology of creation and on a spirituality of the heart, I still had not fully understood the sig-nificance of the embodiment of that theology and spirituality – the book of the body. Even though I have championed the role of the heart in breaking through into a richer meaning of lived revelation, I had not realised the paramount importance of the role of the body in that breakthrough. Even though I have been driven and drawn by the sheer humanity of God, the raw flesh-ing of the Word, the total incarnation of divine love, my head still ruled the roost of my life.

Of all the blessed and possible places in the world, it is here in the snow-white, flat, unassuming reaches of Minnesota, that I am discovering a lost chord which is essential to the music of the lived, abundant life. The human body is the hinge of salvation, according to Tertullian. It is God's masterpiece – the divine work of art. It is only through the body that God's best secrets are revealed. Maryann, just home from the Cameroons, was telling me today, that in the pidgin English for the Angelus, we find 'And the Word He been take man skin'. God delights in being visible and tangible in human skin. The Blessed Trinity dwells deep within our bodies. We believe in the real presence of the body and blood in the eucharist. Yes, we know it all. In fact the Catholic Church, in its most reliable but mostly forgotten tradition, insists on the bodiliness and complete humanness of Jesus Christ and of all of us, both on earth and in heaven. But somehow we have spiritualised beyond recognition, as though the incarnation had never happened, the unique, vital and essential role of the body in our salvation; we have theorised it to a safe distance from the God-given passions of flesh and blood, to a place where it can be held under complete control. Somewhere along the way we have thrown away the body-clock that brings God's work to full time.

In *Breather* One, I wish to address a few points that will be picked up again in the course of our reflections. These points, about how we see our bodies, can serve only as an introduction to a new life-long awareness. So what better way to begin the challenging journey into new territories of our mystery than by befriending our bodies, our estranged companions, and realising, with clarity, that they are, in fact, our safe and faithful home for our entire lives. We bring them everywhere with us, and they take us to all kinds of inside and outside experiences, and yet we know so little about them. We may have names for parts of the body, some facts and information about how they function, where to go for repairs and alterations, but do we truly love and nurture the amazing mystery that our bodies are? Are we aware of the vibrant stories being told inside our bodies and of the dialogue between the inner and outer experiences in relation to our whole person?

Contemporary culture, fuelled by the advertisers and many dubious chat-show role-models, persuade us to conform to the outer images of what our bodies are supposed to look like. If neglecting, misusing, abusing and bludgeoning our own bodies were a crime, most of us would be in jail. We glorify, for instance, the condition of thinness (except where our hair is concerned) and deny the ageing process. Like a difficult object that needs adjusting, we force, contort, starve and punish our bodies out of their natural shape at any given decade of our lives. We are the masters and controllers; our bodies are the victims.

This manipulation began a long time ago. Through training-techniques in childhood; through repression of emotions such as righteous rage and grief because of the perceived code of

behaviour at the time; through the re-direction of sexual energy
and anger to support religious and cultural convention, we have
closed down on the intimate rapport between mind and body.
Small wonder that we have become strangers to our bodies; that
we often hate them. Many of us, who were brought up in a
Catholic environment some decades ago, were subjected to terrible stories and explanations about original sin and about our
bodies, with their devilish tricks for leading us into sin. I have
long since come to see this indoctrination, this castration of
pleasure, as a kind of blasphemy against the awesome Artist of
our exquisitely beautiful bodies.

And so, to be able to travel lightly and joyfully on the journey
ahead, with all our energies flowing in balance, with body, mind
and spirit dancing in rhythm and singing in tune, most of us need
a conversion so as to enjoy our bodies. We need a re-education in
listening to their wisdom, an awareness of the ability of the
nervous system to sense and monitor our inner states, because it
is these unfelt, unheard whispers that have such an immense
influence on our outer condition and that carry the key to our
true fulfilment. These *Breathers* will help the wisdom of the body
to heal us when we accept and experience our feelings, especially
the negative ones. True self-love, and only then the love of our
neighbour, comes about when we develop and honour the feeling capacity. When we begin to believe that the body is in the
soul rather than the soul in the body, and when we come alive to
our senses and to our skin, and see them as guides and transmit-
ters of energy and grace, our whole lives can be transformed.

And God said:
May you delight in your body.
It is my body too.

May you see the world anew each day:
how else can I behold my beauty?
May you fill the earth with the sounds of life:
how else can I hear my song?

May your skin rejoice in the passion of the sun;
and your tongue tingle with the joy of new wine.
Don't you know you are my senses?   Without your
body I cannot be.[5]

Praxis 1

Begin the awareness work today. Sit down for a few minutes and relax. Pay attention to your breathing. Then try to become more aware of your body. Notice the sensations in its different parts. Can you experience your feet inside your shoes, your clothes against your skin, your back against the chair? Is your jaw locked tight? Which parts can you feel at this very moment? Can you tell how your body is affected by your feelings of stress, anxiety or anger? Throughout the day, and the next few days, gently bring your mind back to your body, along these lines. Gradually you will notice a new relaxation and ease about you. You will sit, stand, move and breathe with more grace, confidence and vitality. Because of our distracted and driven nature, our thoughts go everywhere. But gently, gently, again and again, the transformation will begin to happen. Even an initial awareness about the unity of our body, mind and spirit may begin a life-long process. Later on you may decide to explore the benefits of a more structured form of body-work and body-awareness such as *yoga, t'ai chi, reiki,* or a programme of stretching and aerobic exercises. In the meantime, try to be as faithful as you can to a daily pattern of mindfulness regarding your body sensations, your breathing, your thoughts and feelings.

Mind your mind

DAY 2

In readiness for 'the journey we must take' we have briefly looked, yesterday, at the need for a sensitive awareness of our body. *Breather* Two is about an equally developed awareness of our mind. This awareness is often called *mindfulness*, an attentiveness that is refined and attuned through meditation. Please do not be daunted by this reflection. All any of us can do is to keep trying to make this *Breather* a part of our life, to make this exercise of awareness a life's habit. Mindful meditation is about being truly yourself, and knowing how present you are to your body, to your whole self and to others. It is about realising that you are on a spiritual path called your life, and that you have a choice about how much energy you put into its direction and how open you are to the unfolding of that life. Regarding the beginning of the journey inward, Jon Kabat-Zinn writes:

> You have to come to it at the right time in your life, at a point where you are ready to listen carefully to your own voice, to your own heart, to your own breathing – just to be present for them and with them, without having to go anywhere or make anything better or different. This is hard work.[6]

While mindfulness is meant to characterise the whole of our lives as the art of conscious living, of mindful action, it reaches a special focus in meditation. Some of its essential dimensions, as the *Breathers* emphasise, include a non-judgemental attitude in the way we pay attention to what is happening, a deep appreciation of the present moment, an openness to the rich possibilities for growth and transformation arising from the inner stillness. Mindfulness is the opposite of taking things for granted. It is aware of the interconnectedness of everyone and everything, and from this awareness springs true compassion. It avoids the deadly tunnel-vision of personal bias, prejudice or expectation. It is about being our authentic, natural self which follows when we begin to notice the masks we wear, the lies that litter our lives, the pretences that we learn at an early age.

As with *Breather* One, the substance of *Breather* Two, also, is essential to each of the *Breathers* in so far as deep awareness is common to them all. For without the central and grounded unity of body and mind, the journey cannot be even attempted. And nobody promised it would be a stroll in a rose garden. While the meditation practice is gentle, nurturing and empowering, it also requires effort and discipline. After much perseverance, I myself can manage only a few minutes of real inner presence to self at a time. We are always thinking. Our mind is like a roller-coaster full of clamouring thoughts. In meditation we stand by its side and simply notice those fast-moving, fast-changing scenes. It is not so much about whether or not we have 'distractions'. Because we always will. It's more to do with how we watch them slide by.

> By being with yourself, by watching yourself in your daily life with alert interest, with the intention to understand rather than to judge, in full acceptance of whatever may emerge, because it is there, you encourage the deep to come to the surface, and enrich your life and consciousness with its captive energies. This is the great work of awareness; it removes obstacles and releases energies by understanding the nature of life and mind.[7]

In mindful meditation we don't actually *do* anything. We just notice, without passing any comment or option. Nor do we have any expectations about improvement or success or having certain feelings of stillness, for instance. 'Just give up any expectations of yourself,' wrote Pema Chodron, 'That is a good description of how to meditate.' Mindful meditation is about letting the mind be as it is, about a deepening awareness of *the way it is* or of the deceptively simple reality that this is it. These last phrases, which lie at the heart of universal mysticism, remind me to re-assure the reader and myself that in the exploration of this countryside of mystery, no one has the full map. No one has a head-start. It is comforting to note that while we, as beginners, are struggling with this received, distilled essence of the religious and cultural wisdom of all time, the life-long saints, monks and mystics, even to their last breath, saw themselves as beginners too. Grounded in body awareness (*Breather* One) and in mind awareness (*Breather* Two), the following twenty nine *Breathers* will bless, with a more vibrant resonance and a more holistic healing, our simple, complex and most wonderful being.

To be this kind of totally relaxed eternal watcher, or timeless witness, requires attention to breathing. In fact the actual experience of *Breather* One and of *Breather* Two is impossible without an awareness of one's breath. It is so important that hopes for success, or desire for improvement, do not intrude on the meditation. The way forward, the path to follow, can only be revealed within our attentive presence to the present moment. The intrepid traveller needs, above all, immense patience in the practice of this kind of meditation. Mindfulness, eventually, will become second nature to us in all our waking hours. But the mind is not easily quietened. The use of what is called the *mantra* is often recommended. The mantra is a word, or phrase, or symbol that soft-focuses the mind without absorbing it. You hold it in your mind's eye, but not too intensely, so as to keep your thoughts from wandering all over the place. Please forgive me if all of this sounds too difficult and too complex. Nothing, in fact, could be more simple. But it does require committed effort. And also remember that many of our wisest and holiest people would say that the contents of this particular *Breather* hold the key to your freedom, your enlightenment and your pure joy.

Praxis 2

Yesterday's praxis can be put into effect at random times throughout the day. Today's praxis too. A continuous mindfulness, or awareness, is the ultimate aim. In the meantime, as I recommended, because of our distractedness and frailty of purpose, we need planned time and place. Set aside a few minutes each day, say ten to fifteen to start with, to sit and focus on your breathing. During this awareness it is essential not to try to change the pattern of your breathing or to interfere with it in any way. Just breathe and let go. Let everything – your breath, yourself, the whole world – be exactly as it is. You have no desire to alter anything. Keep your mind relaxed – flowing and free. Notice your breathing when the mind is still and when it wanders, stringing the moments of awareness together, breath by breath. Count them if you like, up to ten; then start again. You may manage only five seconds or five minutes. Your concentration may need a little fine-tuning. Yet it is remarkable how swiftly we can slip into that timeless space and, in no time at all, recover a lost joy and find sufficient peace to see us through.

Know your ego

DAY 3

Like many others, I suppose, I have always carried a great fear of public disgrace. At a time when so many of my brother priests are in the news for the wrong reasons, I often wonder when my turn will come! And on the morning when it does, and the Sunday papers are carrying the details, will I turn up for Mass, as usual, and face the parishioners? And if I do, will they point the finger of blame or forgive, frown accusingly or embrace compassionately? Well, last week, a small version of it came suddenly into my life, like a freak wave behind an unsuspecting rower. I place this *Breather* Three at the beginning of the book because it gathers up much of the human condition of shadow and light, that we will touch on during the month ahead.

Before a group of about thirty people, I was stripped of my public face, my dignity and self-respect. Even though it was in the context of a holistic and healing week, and even though everyone present was battling with their own demons, it was still a shock to the system. With the precision of a surgeon, and the finesse of a sculptor, my carefully crafted covers, masks and shells were ruthlessly removed, to reveal a very wounded, unfinished and unprotected inner creature. It seemed like an un-provoked assault, a careless and costly risk that could have done much damage to someone as vulnerable and fragile as myself. There were some of those present who immediately sprang to my defence. It was, nevertheless, and undoubtedly, a classic moment of humiliation.

In his first book about the Enneagram, Richard Rohr explains that, to keep us moving in the right direction along the way of the inner journey of self-knowledge and self–awareness, very often some kind of public shaming has to happen. There is a stage in what is often called the *Work* (of seeking holiness, en-lightenment) that the Sufis call *malamat*. Malamat means blame, failure, discredit, disgrace and humiliation. One story says that while there is a way of purification based on *malamat*, yet, out-side the gates of enlightenment where the people queue to enter heaven, the shortest queue is the one marked '*Malamat*'. One day, most of us who are open to God, must stand for a while in this queue. I have often wondered about so many holy people who have been petrified with fear as some devastating revelation (true or false) about their private lives was about to be made. When this eventually happens, and the person's 'sins' become the headlines of the local or national papers, some just fade out of life and die, their souls crushed forever. Others, the final barrier of human respect and dependence on their good name now broken, begin to blossom. I think of Cardinal Bernardin. It is said that he had two great fears in his life – the fear of disgrace and the fear of cancer. He was challenged on both fronts. He faced those twin terrors with immense grace and trust. And so, his close friends tell us, he reached a unique moment of freedom and peace before he died.

And now, a week later, after my own small taste of public exposure, I like to think that I, too, reacted with dignity and courage. I tried to 'breathe in' to my confusion and hurt, and to call to my aid as many of the following *Breathers* as I could remember. To my credit, for instance, I did not lash back in anger; I did not sulk in silence; and I did not brood or scheme about subtle ways of getting even, later. I was very conscious that there was no malice intended, no personal vendetta, no desire to hurt. This was my teacher teaching me. And teachers, like angels, often come in disguise. Throughout the most intense part of the 'lesson', which lasted for two days, I had an overwhelming sense of being safe, of being held and protected by love. I knew there were faithful friends who truly wanted me to move along my chosen path, but who realised, too, that when the path entered the dark forest, I would become very frightened. They were the ones who held me.

I'm sure the whole incident marks a most important threshold in my breakthrough into a greater degree of authenticity and inner authority. What took a beating was my ego. The ego, as discussed in the Introduction, is the ambiguous, subtle, conscious self that can be a tyrant or a friend. Usually it is a tyrant, a garrulous, devious and false sense of self, a confusing and ensnaring charlatan-self, a most powerful imposter that usurps the reality of the true self. It is the cause of our suffering, our anxieties and fears.

So long as we haven't unmasked the ego, it continues to hoodwink us, like a sleazy politician endlessly parading bogus promises, or a lawyer constantly inventing ingenious

lies and defences, or a talk-show host going on and on talking,
keeping up a stream of suave and emptily convincing chatter, which actually says nothing at all . . . Again and again
we cave in to its demands with the same sad self-hatred as
the alcoholic feels reaching for the drink that he knows is
destroying him, or the drug addict groping for the drug that
she knows after a brief high will only leave her flat and desperate. To end the bizarre tyranny of ego is why we go on the
spiritual journey, but the resourcefulness of ego is almost
infinite and it can at every stage sabotage and pervert our
desire to be free of it.[8]

During those days of painful purification I began to understand how all-embracing and far-reaching the control of the ego
is in my life. As I observed and filtered my thoughts and emotions, my reactions and spontaneous responses to situations, I
saw that almost all my conscious activities were quite simply
ego-driven. Whether it emerged as considerations of self-
importance, fear, vanity, good name, self-protection, the common good, there was no denying the underlying reality – these
were the self-righteous, seductive or craven voices of a dominant,
deceptive ego. After what seemed like a major set-back in my
carefully crafted self-esteem, I now recognise the piercing of my
armour, that day, as a gift from the gods. How else would I ever
know the right valley in which to till the soil, the appropriate
well in which to unblock the source of living water, the one
bright field that held the treasure? There are no easily-obtained,
ready-made maps with such addresses and directions. Only
prayer and suffering draw the soul to them. This is Rumi's advice:

> Put what salve you have on yourself.
> Point out to everyone the disease you are.
> That's part of getting well.
> When you lance yourself that way,
> you become more merciful and wiser.

And yet, in spite of all the chatter and clamour relentlessly
going on during our waking and sleeping hours, we still retain
the memory of our real nature, with all its gentle strength and
clarity. Our true self may have been forced into hiding, exiled
out of its native home, or bombarded by louder voices. But our
true self is a wise guide.

The more often you listen to this wise guide, the more easily you will be able to change your own negative moods, see through them, and even laugh at them for the absurd dramas and ridiculous illusions that they are. Gradually you will find yourself able to free yourself more and more quickly from the dark emotions that have ruled your life, and this ability to do so is the greatest miracle of all. Terton Sogyal, the Tibetan mystic, said that he was not really impressed by someone who could turn the floor into the ceiling or fire into water. A real miracle, he said, was if someone could liberate just one negative emotion.[9]

It is true enough to say that the main goal of today's healers, counsellors, therapists and self-help remedies, and of yesterday's religious practices and penances, was, and still is, the awareness and taming of the ego, the identifying and owning of the passions, the naming and transformation of the seven deadly sins. In a sense, that, too, is the aim of this book. *Breather* Three is about ending the reign of the oppressors of our souls; it is about stopping being victims of the egotistical tapes that keep playing inside our head; it is about enjoying the freedom of God's children and playing, carefree, around the garden of our Mother. Without a searing honesty and trust, this dream will never come true. In one of his weekly columns, Ronald Rolheiser tries to blow our cover:

The discipline of the heart makes us stand in the presence of God with all we have and are; our fears and anxieties, our guilt and shame, our sexual fantasies, our greed and anger, our joys, successes, aspirations and hopes, our reflections, dreams and mental wanderings, and most of all our people, family, friends and enemies – in short all that makes us who we are . . . We tend to present to God only those parts of ourselves with which we feel relatively comfortable and which we think will invoke a positive response. Thus our prayer becomes very selective, narrow and unbalanced. And not just our prayer but also our self-knowledge, because by behaving as strangers before God we become strangers to ourselves.

Praxis 3

It is important to find a special, comfortable place for your sitting and praying. Try not to rush it. If you can spare but for a few
minutes, honour those minutes with your best energy. Gently
distance yourself from the stream of thoughts and anxieties that
are already desperately trying to attract your attention. Notice
the regular beating of your heart. Today, reflect on your feelings
and reactions at times of criticism, disapproval or rejection.
These are the moments when the ego and its tricks are evident.
Notice the denial, the defence, the self-pity that immediately
rush in. This, in fact, goes on all the time and makes our lives in-
authentic and miserable. Notice too our reaction to praise, to
winning, to being proved right. We are over the moon, so very
happy. The ego is having a field-day in both instances. These
examples mean that we are finding our identity only in our
achievements, our possessions and the approval of others. It is
to see our worth only through the eyes of others; to be over-
dependent. There is no inner centre, no grounded self. The journey
ahead is about becoming less self-centred, less touchy and prickly,
less gullible and fearful. But for the moment, just pay particular
attention to the self-importance of the ego on the stage of today's
experiences, whether these be positive or negative. And don't
forget to enjoy the show!

Grow by subtraction

DAY 4

'I make myself rich by making my wants few', wrote Thoreau. There is all the difference in the world between abundance and sufficiency or 'enoughness'. In *Breather* Four we are encouraged to 'let go' of almost everything. Traditionally, this spiritual exercise used to be called 'detachment'. This is an extremely difficult habit to acquire. It is not so much about urgent effort as about trusting surrender; not so much something we do from time to time but, if we can manage it, something that becomes a condition of our daily living. It is a most powerful grace. It is about the emptying and self-stripping that the Book of Life is always placing before us. Letting go and acceptance contain the key to happiness. All our suffering, according to Zen wisdom, comes from attachment to things. Most of our disappointments come from unmet desires and expectations. *Breather* Four whispers, 'Just let go for a minute. Do not torture yourself with these fearful, angry, hopeless thoughts. Take a few big sighs. Trust in God. Don't panic. All will be well because everything passes. So for the moment, just let go.'

There is no end to letting go. Like the ever-falling Minnesota snow outside my window this morning, there is never a moment when there is not something or someone to let go of. And just as often as the snow is cleared away, the empty space is immediately filled up again, so too with our needy and acquisitive nature. No sooner have we let go of one particularly 'necessary' material, spiritual or physical habit or possession than another equally and personally attractive 'necessity' takes its place. At this place we are at the core of our dis-ease. We feel an immense freedom, then, a real salvation, once we allow ourselves to be blessed with the grace of detachment, of letting go, of stopping being a victim of our own or someone else's expectations and emotions. While the quality of detachment is never easy, it does become easier with practice. It is important, also, for us beginners to remember that we will always experience negative feelings about ourselves and others. Even Jesus experienced doubt, disappointment, fear and anger. Negativity is, and will always be, a definition of the human condition. What matters is what happens once we become aware of these feelings. Do we indulge them and wallow in them? Do they cripple and stifle us? Or, as soon as possible, by non-judgementally acknowledging them, do we disarm them, and thus transform them?

I never fail to experience a profound stirring of freedom every time this happens to me. Nevertheless, because of the initial distrust, fear and panic it brings, letting go is a kind of dying, but a dying into a Christ-won liberation. Nobody finds it easy to be stripped, to be emptied, least of all God in becoming human as a defenceless baby or Jesus in his broken and spent body on the cross. It is too risky. But that's what love does – it keeps letting go; and the reward is immense. It is like sinking beneath the stormy waves, like the tempestuous Peter, only to find a new security for your flailing feet, as he did – a new power and ground for your soul. This power gives birth to the miraculous, transfiguring energy of God, allowing you to experience it and releasing it so that those around you become aware of a healing energy. There is no need for arduous, penitential, spiritual exercises. Just by letting go, in trust, into the mystery of God's unconditional love for us, the unblocking of our divinity happens, and resurrection powers its way through the world of hearts and the heart of the world. The clouds rain, the sun shines, the earth surrounds, the farmer sleeps and, with nobody pushing it, the hidden seed is splendidly, effortlessly and irrevocably transformed into its perfect praise.

The practice of letting go is a most difficult and daunting exercise. It can also be an exhilarating one. It applies to our emotions as well as to our possessions. I sometimes find myself doing it many times even in one conversation. Only today, for instance, I felt ignored, then unappreciated and finally I felt quite awkward over something I was unable to accomplish, in company. Almost as quickly as these things happened I let them go, fairly easily and completely. I haven't even thought about them again until this moment. Now if the relief and new energy that flows from handling a daily experience in this way is so significant, think of the deep empowerment that comes when we succeed in letting go of old and new grudges, long-term and recent fears, debilitating and self-destructive bitterness and hatred. As all the books about it testify, letting go is so simple, so demanding and so unbelievably healing and life-giving. Once you have awakened to this awareness, it is difficult not to be changed forever. Our soul, in spite of a mysterious resistance, is coded for this kind of spiritual growing.

Praxis 4

As you settle for meditation, clear your mind of the challenges
and demands of the day ahead. Let peace into your heart, mind
and body. Today's focus is our possessiveness, our clinging, our
hoarding nature. Once you are settled, make a decision to let go
of something today. Begin with an object that's been hanging
around the house, unused, for a while. And I don't mean something useless. Then, in your mind, move on to something else;
something you're holding on to in case it might be needed one
day – a book you've borrowed, a special postcard you've never
used, a brooch or tie you haven't worn for years. Go through the
house. In your imagination, first, give many things away. Don't
do it for a gift in return. Let go of something every few days. It
brings a great feeling after the initial struggle. It brings immense
power and wealth. Later on we will try to let go of the negative
emotions about which we have just reflected. In the meantime,
during the minutes you are devoting to meditation, or at other
times of the day, practise 'letting go' with every exhalation in
your breathing. Every time you breathe out, visualise parting
with one of your possessions or even one of your quite hidden
and self-justified prejudices. Even though in a small way, this is
still a kind of dying. Jesus died many 'little deaths' before his
final letting go. And each death, however insignificant, brings
its own abundant resurrection.

Take the second take

DAY 5

Another image and wise thought that has helped me continually and immensely is found in *Breather* Five. It has to do with perspective. Can you remember when some insignificant comment or event not only upset you at the time but for the whole day or even week? While an aware part of us realises how silly it is to allow ourselves to be victimised by a passing, negative blip, another dimension of our psyche is undefended and helpless. I have often felt so angry with myself for allowing some truly unimportant remark to colour my mood for a ridiculously long time; especially when I believe that, in most situations, no one can hurt us without our permission. Buddhist teaching reminds us that, while ignoring quite important issues in our lives, we blow small things up out of all proportion. Our response is totally inappropriate to the stimulus. 'We often add to our pain and suffering,' the Dalai Lama reminds us, 'by being overly sensitive, overreacting to minor things, and sometimes taking things too personally . . .' Therapists often refer to this narrowing of our psychological field of vision as a self-inflicted 'personalising of our pain'. For those who are victims of this mental trap, every comment and encounter can become a potential source of misery.

The arrival of appropriate perspective brings a restored balance to our thinking and feeling. This *Breather* asks, 'Are you over-reacting? Is it truly that bad? Taking the long view, how awful is it, really? In fact, in the cold light of day, does it, in fact, merit all that intense emotion?' The wise people tell us that the recovery of perspective is the first strategy in regaining our emotional balance so as to react maturely. Caught off guard, through some kind of frightened tunnel-vision, our focus shrinks and we lose the wider view. We forget that in the awful scale of the disasters that happen around us, our own particular worry, loss or fear is usually very small indeed. It becomes, in fact, quite insignificant. But because of some weakness of the spirit, some self-centred, ego-driven exaggeration, we find ourselves stuck in a life-destroying imbalance.

I have often felt so sad at the fact that innumerable people in the second half of their lives are consumed with bitterness and self-destroying, deep-seated emotions over previous lost opportunities, broken hearts, deceits and betrayals. The persistent and penetrating negative forces shape their very bodies. They have *become* the hatred, the loss, the hopelessness. A time comes, I believe, when, in such instances, it takes small miracles of loving to bring back wholeness. At a more everyday level, however, we need the second take on the reason for our premature panic because the first reaction is usually thoughtless, groundless and irrational. In the realisation that we have unthinkingly and inappropriately *become* the reaction, the healing happens. Because of the miracle of its power, we will return again to this unhooking of ourselves from the bait of our ego in future *Breathers*, eg Praxis 31.

There is no need for complicated antidotes and undoings. Once we separate ourselves from the hurting feelings, once we resist identifying with the anger or jealousy or revenge, then in that very separating and detaching, the recovery almost instantly takes place. It is so important to understand this. This *Breather* alone can bring immense peace and freedom to tortured souls. The Dalai Lama has often said that 'We don't need more money, we don't need greater success or fame, we don't need the perfect body or the perfect mate; right now, at this very moment, we have a mind, which is all the basic equipment we need to achieve complete happiness.' The Christian would interpret 'Buddha mind' here as 'the mind of Christ' which St Paul entreats us to 'put on'.

Baptised, redeemed and continuously graced as we are, we still keep forgetting that we have a free choice in the encounters and happenings of each day. I can choose to be grateful, for instance, even when parts of me are steeped in hurt and resentment. It is amazing, too, how many opportunities present themselves when I can choose gratitude instead of complaint. I can choose to be grateful, for example, when I'm criticised, even when a part of my heart is responding with bitterness. I can choose to speak about goodness and beauty, even when part of me is looking for someone to blame or for something to call ugly. I can choose to listen to my inner voices that forgive, and express it outwards with smiling eyes, even while I still hear whispers of revenge echoing in one of the empty halls of my heart. Today you will have many occasions to take the second take!

Praxis 5

At meditation today, try to make your being still by paying attention to the physical feelings and sensations of your body and
the thoughts and images in your mind. Notice the pattern of
your breathing as you exhale and inhale slowly and mindfully.
As you feel the peace flowing through you, gently anticipate the
challenges that will try to take it from you the moment you leave
this place of prayer. It is very probable that someone will 'press
your buttons' today. Visualise the particular person who is likely
to say something hurtful, harsh or cutting to you. When this
happens, you can be sure that you will initially feel the sudden,
negative emotion of anger, embarrassment or fear. Even the
most enlightened saints reacted like that. But almost immediately,
they became aware of what was happening in them and they
allowed the emotion to die away. They did not recycle the negativity back to its source. They 'breathed into it' and, with a fine
and blessed strength, they let it go. This transformation, this
alchemy, is a kind of spiritual miracle. And, because Jesus said
so, you too can achieve that miracle. And it is so important not to
be disheartened if you feel that you are making little headway.
No effort goes waste. Even our failures are harvested by God.
And through it all, the healing and the purifying continue to
grace our lives.

Notice the grace of space

DAY 6

On certain days the rut is very deep; too deep to climb out over the slippery, slidy slopes. We are enveloped in anxious thoughts; our emotions are lifeless. At such times I'm not a very nice person to know. It feels as if I'm rendered powerless in some kind of oppressive fog. And then I become aware that I have a choice. I imagine a line running across my mind, separating my thoughts. Below the line are the murky waters of fretting, frustration and fear. Above the line is where the positive and hopeful things live. It is here that I make a decision. It is not an easy one. I can remain a victim of my own negativity and descend into the self-perpetuating distress of the hurt ego, or I can leap out of that swampy rut on to the firm and energy-giving ground of positive thinking and letting go. This is now a tested habit that brings me untold relief, time after time. It is like escaping from a suffocating cellar into God's fresh air. *Breather* Six is about remembering the grace of space.

We forget to allow our souls to expand into the infinity of God. There is nothing that can threaten or frighten us when God is on our side. If God be for us, who can be against? 'I can do all things in Christ who sets me free.' At unprepared times of fearful pressure and anxious stress, I fill my mind with images of the hugeness of the ocean, the vastness of the sky, remembering that God's power is as immense as these and is at my disposal right here and right now. (Billions of galaxies, for instance, are 150,000 light years in diameter!) So, together with a friend, we have devised a strategy for dancing from the trap of negative or depressing thoughts. We call it 'the wiggle-waggle' technique. That is like the minnow or the salmon which, when danger threatens, with a few gracefully-powerful flicks of the tail, slip away into the free spaces. They even use the constrictions of their situation to propel themselves out of reach. And so can we. We have a choice, a vital alternative. We can opt for the grace of space, acting out of our authentic, divine self, or we can refuse to grow, remaining a victim of the fear that surrounds our false self.

There is a mysterious healing-space in the Irish version of set-dancing. The ritualistic weaving around and escaping between others, the little jumps and quick turns, the circling and swooping, the diving beneath a couple's arms into new free space to meet and face the next row of dancers, is a lovely image to carry at those times of feeling constricted by the rut we allow ourselves to fall into. This *Breather* is about the many unexplored escape routes we have at our disposal for transforming and transcending the cellars and graves we build around our frightened hearts; it is about graced ways of experiencing God's intoxicating blessings freely offered since the final breakthrough of Jesus.

As the dancer avoids colliding by a sense of graceful rhythm, as the water is guided by the river-banks to the sea, or the toboggan, by glancing off the hard sides of the icy run, hurtles to the finishing line, we, by bouncing against the familiar edges of our negative tendencies, and without getting snagged up in them, can learn to experience the life-giving grace of shifting into the place of no fear. Often and often I have relied on this to speed me on my way into the enemy-free zones of positive places. It is a matter of deliberate decision. Why linger in the dark and shadowy shallows where only our fears and hurts are lurking? There is a sacred space where true transformation happens. I never tire of reflecting on R. S.Thomas' *Via Negativa*.

Why no! I never thought other than
That God is that great absence
In our lives, the empty silence
Within, the place where we go
Seeking, not in the hope to
Arrive or find. He keeps the interstices
In our knowledge, the darkness
Between the stars. His are the echoes
We follow, the footprints he has just
Left. We put our hands in
His side hoping to find
It warm. We look at people
And places as though he had looked
At them, too; but miss the reflection.[10]

I like to link grace, space and energy. This *Breather* is simply following scriptural advice to fill our minds with large and mind-expanding images of infinite light and things eternal. Left to ourselves, we tend to dig ourselves (and God) into lifeless ruts and deadly graves. According to Answer 21 in the *Penny Catechism* of our childhood, God is everywhere – within us and around us. God, St Thomas assures us, is 'pure spirit' and 'sheer joy'. That is why there is a pulsing energy at our innermost centre. As the strings of the violin are stretched and pitched to true tone, our life's work is to be tuned in to these divine vibrations. The Word of God is whispered from our centre, bringing a lightness and a lift to all we experience. The abundant life is from inside out. The holy shrine of power and energy is found within our hearts. Nothing is impossible anymore. According to St Paul, we are already becoming 'copies of the glorious body of God'. And the light and the energy flow through us and from us. In that space and dimension of existence, we are always new, always young, always shining.

Praxis 6

Every thought and feeling we have affects the condition of our body. When I ask that, at your moment of prayer this morning, you call to mind some situation or relationship that bothers you, do you notice a change in your heartbeat, a tightening of some part of your body (which part?), a difference in your breathing? Just notice; that is enough. Now every time you exhale, hand over this concern to God, to the Life and Love that is within and around us, who is all-powerful and who loves us unconditionally. In spite of your doubts, make a huge act of faith. I believe, O Lord, help my unbelief. When you pray from your inmost heart like this – those good old-fashioned prayers – the infinite forces of goodwill and compassion are already working on what is worrying you. The angels appointed to us – to oversee every relationship and to remove everything that blocks our path to God – are already at full stretch. As the river knows about flowing, the rose about blooming, and as our bodies know about healing, so too, the life-force, the universal energy of Being, has begun its holy work within us. Whenever a moment presents itself during the next few hours, calm your breathing, move inside yourself, and simply renew the surrender of your current, particular anxiety to your Tremendous Lover.

Dance the dance

DAY 7

At the school nativity play, the children on the wings can't wait for their moment of glory as they impatiently shift and shuffle for their turn under the spotlight. Or, for instance, in another image, one by one the instruments of the orchestra have their part to play, now in full sound, now silent. So too with the family of sub-personalities within each one of us. When this phenomenon of my different faces and personas was first revealed to me, it made an awful lot of sense. It brought me much peace and a better understanding of my often-strange behaviour. At one time, for example, the holy one would want to emerge and swagger during some meeting or other, or maybe all day; at another time, the hunter, the rebel, the seducer, the warrior, the destroyer, the wild man and so on. *Breather* Seven is about the identity of the community-member of our heart that comes to strut, grovel, threaten or bless on stage each morning of a new day.

Imagine a wheel, the hub of which is the grounded, centred self, and the spokes are the sub-personalities, the faces, the masks, the roles and defences we call upon and use every day. The wheel bumps along over the uneven road of our lives, and with every jolt we unconsciously shift the image from spoke to spoke, from sub-personality to sub-personality. We seem committed to going round in circles, making it very difficult to begin in a new place. Most of us are in this circular rut. It is only our persistent sense of awareness that will save us; only our space to choose that will set us free; only our paradigm shift from ego to essence, from false self to true self, that will reveal the basic pattern of our hopes and fears. Many of my friends have admitted to a profound relief when the world of sub-personalities was opened up to them. If Thoreau is right when he holds that 'the unexplored life is not worth living', then the ranking of our inner community, the pecking-order of our sub-personalities, must be among the first to be encountered.

However, just recently, I have been helped by noticing my reactions and behaviour, not so much in terms of multiple sub-personalities, but in terms of two basic attitudes. Some spiritual

writers tell us that on any given occasion we react to the events
and encounters of our day, either out of what they call the *anima
magna* or the *anima pussila*. The former is the seat of bigness,
goodness, compassion, all things magnanimous and generous.
The latter is the source of meanness, smallness, all things narrow
and shrivelled. It is within our power to handle the daily challenges
of life from either of these positions. This has huge consequences
for the quality of our job-satisfaction, family relationships and life
in general. So often we allow others to decide our mood, sometimes for the whole day. A rude gesture from a motorist, a snide
comment from a work-colleague, a reproving look from a member of the family and we seem defenceless to get back into our
previously happy frame of mind.

It does not have to be like that. We have substantial control
over our moods if we but believe it. It is one of the self-support-
ing techniques of many of today's healers, exponents of positive
thinking, and spiritual gurus who are heavily into the power of
repeated affirmations. We find St Paul, like Jesus, exhorting us
to keep our minds on 'the higher things' such as goodness, truth
and beauty. 'Finally, sisters and brothers, fill your minds with
everything that is true, everything that is noble, everything that
is good and pure, everything that we love and honour, everything that can be thought beautiful and worthy of wonder.' (Phil
4:7) They were totally convinced that the positive was always
stronger than the negative. 'You were darkness once, but now
you are light; be like children of light.' (Eph 5:8) The Dalai Lama,
too, is a great believer in the mind's two faces – the chosen look
of unredeemed fallenness and its consequent attitudes, and the
chosen look that transcends and eliminates its afflictions by
thinking and feeling compassion and forgiveness.

This *Breather* brings relief because it reminds us not to be
shocked at what we discover going on inside us. A misleading
kind of religious teaching or preaching would have us believing
that only angels should inhabit our hearts. Nobody told us that
forever and a day, the demons would be in there too. There is a
kind of suppression, in childhood, of the dark dimension of our
psyche, that in later years wreaks havoc with our sanity and
peace of mind. There is a divine spark in the worst of us and a
powerful evil in the best of us. And they are closely intertwined.
You cannot pull out the badness, leaving the goodness intact,
anymore than you can pull out the weeds, as Jesus reminded his

friends, without damaging the healthy plants. The wise old warrior Alexander Solzhenitsyn wrote:

> If only it were all so simple! If only there were evil people
> somewhere insidiously committing evil deeds, and it were
> necessary only to separate them from the rest of us and de-
> stroy them. But the line dividing good and evil cuts through
> the heart of every human being. And who is willing to de-
> stroy a piece of his own heart?[11]

Rainer Maria Rilke believed that if he got rid of his demons,
his angels might also leave. In a lovely and thought-provoking
passage, he writes 'Perhaps all the dragons in our lives are
princesses who are only waiting to see us act, just once, with
beauty and courage. Perhaps everything terrible is, in its deepest essence, something helpless that needs our love.' That is why
I called this *Breather* 'Dance the Dance' (of Light and Shadow).

That 'one act of beauty and courage' will have something to
do with risking our own happiness by dying for others; with
giving over our lives in the service of our neighbour. Doing
'something beautiful for God' is a liberating decision because
our hearts are made to be given away. There are as many ways
of crossing over from a preoccupation with self to an authentic
concern for others, as there are willing people. It is the ultimate
pass-over, but a bridge too far for most of us. Always trying to
'do the loving thing', always trying to put someone else first, always being aware of the temptations of the false self, not only
brings abundant life and health to our present human condition,
but also is the swiftest way home to God. No less a role-model
than Archbishop Oscar Romero left us this piece of wisdom before his murder:

> The guarantee of one's prayer is not in saying a lot of words.
> The guarantee of one's petition is very easy to know:
> How do I treat the poor?
> – because that is where God is.
> The degree to which you approach them –
> that is how you approach your God.
> The way you look at them is the way you look at God.

Praxis 7

Once you have begun your meditation, and are firmly comfortable in your sitting position, start again to watch the play of thoughts, feelings and sensations within you. This witnessing already provides a necessary detachment from them. Notice the stillness, and listen to the beating of your heart. Your shoulders drop and your breathing becomes calmer and slower. When anxieties arise about the day ahead, thoughts about the way you may be misunderstood, crossed or put down, notice the anger, impatience, resolutions and fear that tense up your body and distract your mind. This will happen again and again. Trustingly let such thoughts slip away. When those moments come during the day, you will see them as opportunities to practise your new way of being present to them. Notice the way you change your attitudes, your presence and your masks as you find yourself in different situations, encountering different people. Just notice. Do not pass mental comments. Listen to your heart and your body. They will tell you to breathe a little deeper, to wait for a moment, to let the hurting incident pass, to act out of your larger self – the angel-self. Even if it is only for a split second, you will discover that there is an instant when you have the chance to choose – between the immediate, negative, thoughtless reaction or the aware response that changes the personal, hurtful charge into a mutually life-giving moment. This is the only loving and wise thing to do.

Paint on a broader canvas

DAY 8

Fellow travellers on the inner quest have shared an important realisation with me – one that afforded them a welcome way of coping when their own load seemed heavy, making the thought of facing another day quite difficult. It has to do with realising that we are, especially in our suffering, simply one person among many in this state called 'life'. In one very important sense, we are not all that important! In fact, after a recent male rite of passage in the high desert of New Mexico, a few other sobering and clarifying insights were impressed upon us. Life is hard. You are going to die. You are not in control. Your life is not about you. They sound pretty hard and uncompromising, but they were offered to us compassionately, with affirmations from the gospels. We spent many hours mulling over them.

My friend John was confiding in me only last week about the morning he felt quite depressed over his domestic circumstances. Like the familiar cloud, his negativity was hanging heavily over him as he set out walking to his office. As he lifted his head he noticed how busy the sidewalks were with so many people going hither and thither with all sorts of expressions on their faces. 'I'm just one of many,' he suddenly and gratefully thought, 'I'm just one of the human race. This is what it's like to be alive. Good days, not-so-good days. Just like everyone else. Why do I expect to be the exception? Why do I expect to be happy every day? I'm no different from anyone else. It's called life.' I too find that kind of thinking immensely liberating. It might, at first, seem like cold comfort, but the tremendous built-in realism never fails to restore some kind of balance to my moods.

Let me take this *Breather* about our shared humanity one step further. 'It is our suffering,' the Dalai Lama reminds us, 'that is the most basic element that we share with others, the factor that unifies us with all living creatures.' My friend John's moment of release from depression and isolation arose from his sense of a common human suffering. There is a 'wound of humanity', a fragility inseparable from the human condition. Now here is one of the universal treasures of wisdom for keeping a level of acceptance and joy in our precarious daily lives. Once John saw himself as part of a struggling world, not alienated from it, an awareness of a deep interconnectedness and interdependence arose within him. In the face of this awareness the human heart can only feel compassion. And compassion is a powerful healer. It takes us out of ourselves. We are fashioned for compassion. We all carry its seeds. When those seeds grow, our inner selves become free.

There are many examples of such experiences on the part of everyday mystics as well as the more famous ones. Thomas Merton, for instance, tells us about the afternoon of March 18th, 1958. At the corner of Fourth and Walnut in down-town Louisville, he was suddenly filled with a sense of identity with the throngs of people around him. It was a kind of peak-moment when his heart was moved to bursting-point with love for each one. He felt he could see them as God saw them and that he himself belonged inseparably with them. He was an integral part of the community of ordinary folk —the human family that was trying to live out the passion, death and resurrection of Jesus as they did their shopping in a Kentucky city on a spring day. This graced moment healed him of the wound of isolation and separation which, as a monk, was greatly concerning him. This feeling of fracture had been with him for nearly twenty years. He often returned to that afternoon with gratitude and joy because it was a threshold moment of freedom and release in his spiritual journey.

Most of our great religions and cultures teach that an openness to our affinity with all human beings and, most importantly, to all of creation too, brings the most sublime gifts of joy. It is a central belief in Buddhism, for example, that when we take upon ourselves, not just our own pain, but a little of the despair and loneliness of our sisters and brothers, then we are saving humanity, and ourselves in the process. There is a Buddhist prayer:

As long as space endures
As long as sentient beings remain
May I too live
To dispel the miseries of the world.[12]

It is also quite explicit in the Christian creed that by uniting our own pain and that of a 'groaning creation' with the passion of Christ, we are finalising here and now, in time and space, God's redemption of the universe. Walking through the streets

of life, with a head and heart full of compassion, changes the
very face of the earth itself. This is the work of angels. Through a
grace-filled empathy and sympathy, all suffering now takes on a
new meaning. Teilhard de Chardin said that if all the world's
pain could be borne in this bonding way, even for an instant, a
fresh new world would be born. We are blessed a hundredfold
for such a hard-won attitude. Our spirits are nourished and a
new energy floods our bodies and minds.

Something incredible is going on in our lives. The whole
story of creation, human and non-human evolution, is somehow
transparent in the lives of the saints and mystics. While there is a
perennial cycle and turning of the seasons always going on, we,
more ordinary mortals, are blessed with glimpses only now and
then. I often think we should sell everything up and take ourselves, our children and our true friends to someplace safe,
where we can all become familiar with mystery, at home with
magic, full of reverence for our experiences of just being.
Physicist Brian Swimme and theologian Richard Rohr talk, in
their own ways, about the revelation of a walk in the forest.
Swimme believes that after such a walk, we are changed forever.
The forest and its life have become a part of us. We emerge, transformed, out into the light. Rohr writes about what happens when
we go through the woods. We see young trees, and we see trees in
their great height and health, and we see dying trees. And somehow, our spirit says, 'I was once a little sapling, but I'm going to be
one of these old trees pretty soon, and that's fine and even good.
I'm part of the Great Wheel, and it's part of the great Paschal mystery, and every day is darkness and light, life and death.'

I was preaching in California and I told them, 'It's dangerous
to live in California, because you don't have the truth that
they have in Minnesota. Minnesota speaks reality better than
Southern California. So don't stay here too long; take a few
trips to Minnesota. Half of life is cold; half of life is scary and
dangerous. Only half is sunny summertime. Together they
make a full cycle. That's the inexorable wheel, the wheel that
we Christians call the Paschal Mystery. It is also good creation
spirituality. Its as solid as the scriptures, it's as solid as the
psalms, it's as solid as St Francis. Once we learn how to see,
how to contemplate, how to let the moon and the sun and
stars and the seasons and the trees and plants and animals
speak to us; once we find our instinctual self in the eyes of
animals, then we are ready . . .[13]

There is an astonishing shift in our attitude to our own work, both inner and outer, when we begin to see it against that infinite horizon, and to our own suffering when we begin to believe in its infinite value for the healing of our sisters and brothers, and of the whole earth, as we fill out and fill in, all that is still incomplete, as Paul puts it, in the work of Jesus Christ. No stranger to pain herself, Sheila Cassidy is familiar with this insight:

I believe no pain is lost.
The blood shed in Salvador
will irrigate the heart of some
financier a million miles away.
The terror, pain, despair, swamped
by lava, flood or earthquake
will be caught up like mist
to fall again, a gentle rain
on arid hearts or souls despairing
in the back streets of Brooklyn.[14]

There is one last elusive insight I want to mention briefly here. It has something to do with the way that all of life, non-human and human, human and divine, created and incarnated, ordinary and mysterious, are all played out, lived through, and personally experienced in each one's life. This *Breather*, about painting on a broader canvas, about seeing our lives against an infinite horizon, about reverencing the sheer mystery and amazing wonder of our own being, and that of all creation, cannot but shift our whole perspective on whatever is currently disturbing our peace.

Praxis 8

To appreciate the stillness and vastness of our world, of the universe, of the cosmos, and of our place within this mystery, we need to become aware of the inner rhythm of our breathing and of our heartbeat. It is one thing to know something about the deeper significance of what we do, 'the infinite horizon' of our daily work; it is another to feel it from within. To sense our own pain in the context of 'the wound of humanity' and to believe more whole-heartedly in the healing of which we are capable, try to follow your breath in the pattern of its ebb and flow. Sit comfortably and surrender your thoughts and images to the sensations of your body and of your breathing. There is no need to deepen the way you inhale or exhale, at this point; the exercise is about becoming aware of the timing of each movement and of the pause in between. There is a quiet similarity here with the turning of the seasons and the rhythm of nature. At these moments of non-doing, our eternal longing for ultimate intimacy is nourished and held by the embrace of God. By persevering in the practice of daily meditation in this way, we hope to reach a way of being where an awareness of the wider context of our experiences is never far from our hearts and minds.

Meet God halfway

DAY 9   In our journey to wholeness, or inner freedom, it is often reassuring to realise that God is also busy seeking us. It is not a lonely one-way enterprise. There are many wise folk who hold that we have already arrived at the place we are striving to reach, that we already have within us the divine qualities we yearn for. But we can never be certain about such things. If we were, we would stop looking too soon. The moment we think we have solved the mystery we are truly lost. Mystery is not like a problem that can be figured out; it is, rather, the unfathomable context of our lives, the infinite backdrop against which we can know anything. The philosopher and theologian Martin Buber reminds us that 'all spiritual journeys have a hidden destination of which the traveller is unaware.' I find it immensely consoling to reflect on the truth that, in the midst of our human conflicts, misfortunes and neuroses, are the pathways along which the Spirit of Life, for which we're searching, is also seeking us. Many centuries ago, the Rhineland mystic Johann Tauler wrote, 'When I say that God seeks man in his house and ransacks it . . . it is as if we had never known anything about God at all. Every idea that we ever had of him, every manifestation of him that we have ever known, will be taken away from us as he searches to find us.'

Most reflective people who are sincere about, and committed to, the inner journey will be aware of this truth. On the one hand, they will be aware that God's ways are not our ways, and that's for sure! – the *Via Negativa*. On the other hand, they will be forever trying to recognise and identify Jesus, the incarnate God, in all the encounters of life – the *Via Positiva*. These would include the turning of the seasons, the awareness of the needy ones who are never far away, the call to enter the place of light and risk. At such moments we strive to believe that the beckoning God of surprises is always searching for us, encompassing us, far more eager to be intimate with us than we are with God. In fact, encouraging as this belief is, the truth is more amazing still. Not only does God come more than halfway to meet us, it is God's own self, in the first place, that moves us to begin the journey. And not only does God inspire us to begin the journey, but it is

God who sustains and nourishes us as we travel. And not only does God sustain us and nourish us as we travel, it is God who carries us when we grow despondent, footsore and weary, finally deciding to give up the quest. It is God who then lies down with us on the night before we, with broken hearts and spirits, prepare to stumble back to where we started from. And it is God, that very same night, who holds us close to her warm body, breathing words of hope and healing into our cold and empty hearts. 'My darling, do you know how much I love you? It is my greatest delight to be looking at you, and to be walking every step of this way with you. Just rest in my arms tonight and tomorrow, when the new light shines, we will continue to dance our way into amazing adventures.' To get to the heart of the matter, to find words that express something of the mutual ecstasy of possession by God, we turn to mystics such as St John of the Cross:

One dark night,
Fired with love's urgent longings
– Ah the sheer grace –
I went out unseen,
My house being now all stilled . . .

On that glad night,
In secret, for no one saw me,
Nor did I look at anything,
With no other light to guide
Than the one that burned in my heart;

This guided me
More surely than the light of noon
To where he waited for me
– him I knew so well –
In a place where no one else appeared.

O guiding night!
O night more lovely than the dawn!
O night that has united
The Lover with his beloved,
Transforming the beloved in her Lover . . .

Upon my flowering breast
Which I kept wholly for him alone,
There he lay sleeping,
And I caressing him,

There in a breeze from the fanning cedars.
When the breeze blew from the turret,
Parting his hair,
He wounded my neck
With his gentle hand,
Suspending all my senses.

I abandoned and forgot myself,
Laying my face on my beloved;
All things ceased; I went out from myself,
Leaving my cares
Forgotten among the lilies.

Our best theologians agree with our greatest mystics. They tell us that there is *nothing* we can do to make headway along the path of bliss. Love does it all. The only power we have is the power to prevent God from loving and saving us. God is the energy and aspiration of our heart and soul. All we can do is block off, resist and reject the divine pleading. And God is not easily put off. Even the disillusionment and despair that kills our beautiful hope can be transformed by God into a pruning and a stripping that forces us to surrender our pride. The challenge for you, in today's *Breather* is to perceive the divine face in the very thoughts and feelings that cloud your heart just now. You rejoice in God's beauty as the evening sun drops low over the horizon; do you equally praise God when your morning spirits drop low over the day ahead? Can you completely transform the heaviness and meaning of the baggage on your back, by accepting it as gift – as key to, and fuel for, your next spiritual mile? Amongst the beautiful secrets that God has revealed to us, this miraculous, life-enhancing alchemy must be the most precious. Of all the *Breathers,* even our fumbling attempts to practise this one meet with an extraordinary transformation in the quality of our lives.

That is why this task is of the essence of the inner journey. It is never completed. Nor is it ever easy. It is all about contradictions and paradoxes. It is, in fact, about loving your enemies, cherishing your wounds, celebrating the very things that trip you up, slow you down, block your path, frustrate and frighten you. Without these threatening happenings or dark memories there can be no healing, growing or travelling. Our enemy is really our precious teacher; that is why Jesus asks us to love our enemy. When someone wishes to harm us we should revere that unique person, according to Buddhist philosophy. It is like finding a precious treasure in answer to our prayers. Our whole being may recoil at this notion of venerating the cause of our misery, yet we are persuaded by the wisdom of the ages that such a difficult approach is the swiftest way to clear vision, spiritual and psychological freedom and true peace. 'All things (even sin) work together for the good of them that love God ...' (Rom 8:28) It is usually in disguise that God comes to meet us; and the disguised God often lives at the strangest addresses. Even Christians have trouble believing that God is absolutely everywhere, despite the irrefutable evidence of the incarnation.

Yours is the light that breaks from the
dark, and the good that sprouts from the deft heart
of strife.

Yours is the gift that still is gain when
everything is a loss, and the life that flows through
the caverns of death.

Yours is the heaven that lies in the common
dust, and You are there for me; You are there
for all.[15]

Praxis 9

When you sit or lie down today for your quiet time, picture the person who is currently giving you the most hassle and grief. As you enter into your inner sanctuary, becoming conscious of your breathing and heartbeat, draw an imaginary circle of light around that person's head. With an open, brave and generous heart, let your negative (and maybe justified) feelings fall away. Reflect on the potential benefits that this person has brought your way – enabling you to feel the size of your soul, to realise that there is nothing you cannot do when empowered by the Holy Spirit. When you bless this person, when you release them from the grip of your anger, your draining energies are restored for life-giving work. You sense the spiritual freedom that suddenly floods your whole being. This is an immense grace. There is probably no higher evidence of our inner divinity. As the day wears on, or maybe when you meet this particular 'thorn in your side', you may experience the same old feelings of anger, revenge or even hatred. Do not be discouraged. The transformation that happened once (though briefly) in your heart, can happen again. Your love and trust and courage has opened the first and most difficult door. But remember, it is almost impossible to keep that inner door of forgiveness open without daily meditation.

Where is your bright face?

DAY 10

Another *Breather* I use at difficult times is about 'breathing in' God's light to transform my darkness. As I sit, or lie on the bed, or walk, I hold my arms out wide (initially only when no one else was about but now I don't really care) and visualise God's power filling my body. I imagine divine energy flooding from my innermost centre, where the Blessed Trinity lives, up into my lungs, veins and heart, pumping through my arteries, carrying and incarnating the divine into every pore and cell along the surface of my skin, bringing to my countenance the 'shine and sheen' that Thomas Aquinas, the greatest Catholic theologian, wrote about. All of this we have on the authority, too, of another spiritual giant who was well aware of his own light and shadow, of his free vision and also of his 'thorn in the flesh'. It was, of course, St Paul who wrote, 'This Lord is the Spirit. Where the Spirit of the Lord is, there is freedom. And we, with our unveiled faces, reflecting like mirrors the brightness of the Lord, all grow brighter and brighter as we are turned into the image that we reflect.' The glowing 'brightness of face' that St Paul has immortalised in his writings, happens when the hidden self, fashioned in God's image, is brought to the surface of our lives.

Describing St Gregory Palamas as one of the 'spiritual stars of the millennium', Bishop Kallistos of Diokleia, a lecturer at Oxford University, goes on to write, 'Believing as he does in the omnipresence of the divine energies, Gregory insists upon the intrinsic holiness of the human body and of the whole material creation. The divine light transfigures the bodies as well as the souls of the saints, so that they themselves become – in both body and soul – that which they behold. As he puts it, "The body is deified along with the soul." What matters to him is that we should each attain, personally and consciously, the vision "face to face" of the living God, and this he believes to be possible not only in heaven but in this present life. It is this that makes him distinctively a theologian for our desacralised era.' (*The Tablet*, 18 March 2000)

I imagine a rainbow of light around my body, a kind of Celtic

65

caim encompassing me. I allow myself to be taken over by the
lightness, brightness and beauty of God. It pulses in my heart, it
flows in my veins, it smiles in my face and comes in and goes out
through my feet, my head and my skin. I pray to become
translucent so that nothing in my heart, mind or body will ever
obscure the radiance and shining of the God within me. I plead
with God for the gift of transparency, that I may be an epiphany
of divine loving. 'Make me a channel of your peace. May I be a
unique sacrament of your compassion, O Lord. Even if I walk in
the valley of darkness, as I do today, burn up within me, the
dead wood of useless anxieties and foolish fears. Fan into living
flames of strength and power, the smouldering embers of the
fire of your heart in mine. I know and believe that it is your
greatest desire to bring about this profound change in me. Even
while I now place all my hope in you, I can feel this transformation taking place.' A friend has just sent me this Celtic benediction:

> May the blessing of
> the Gatherer of Hope
> the Bringer of Springtime
> the Brightener of Seasons
> be upon you as you set forth today.
>
> Laughter of the running hours be yours.
> Lightness and joy be yours.
> And may the blessing of the Triune God
> protect you and guide you.

There is nothing without God's light and lightness. When
drawing out the wisdom of *Breather* Ten, I reflect on the cosmic
unity of all things. Because Christianity has always been the
greatest champion of a mystical intimacy at the heart of nature,
of the universal indwelling of the Holy Spirit of energy, of the
brightness of the divine artist in everything that exists, it is a pity
that so many fearful Christians resist embracing this most energy-
giving and spirit-quickening truth. There is a stream of light
holding all things in creative tension and flow. Poets like Dylan
Thomas keep this doctrine alive:

> The force that through the green fuse drives the flower
> Drives my green age . . .
> The force that drives the water through the rocks
> Drives my red blood.[16]

One bright day the world will wake up from its nightmares of greed and avarice, its mad self-destruction and inhuman evil, and, just in time, the holiness of universal energy will be reverenced. The planet earth will be revered as the Child of God and the Mother of Life. The harsh dualism of religious dogmas and profit-crazed power-brokers will be transformed by a deeper life-force that will transform our blind addictions into true vision. 'One bright day, and make it soon, O Lord of Love, O Woman of Life, breathe a new and loving wisdom into our ignorant and selfish hearts. Restore them to their true image and wonder – the image and wonder of you.'

To place oneself in the middle of what Tagore calls the *Stream of Life* is to feel a new power and perspective, and to find a heartening confidence in the current of one's destiny, even with all its nooks and crannies, down all our days and nights:

The same stream of life that runs through my veins
night and day runs through the world
and dances in rhythmic measures.
It is the same life that shoots in joy through the dust of the earth
in numberless blades of grass
and breaks into tumultuous waves of leaves and flowers.
It is the same life that is rocked
in the ocean-cradle of birth and of death, in ebb and flow.
I feel my limbs made glorious by the touch of this world of life.
And my pride is from the life-throb of ages
dancing in my blood this moment.[17]

Praxis 10

When settled in your position for prayer today, begin as usual to let go of every thought and distraction, shift into the inside place, attend to the moment-to-moment unfolding of the 'here and now' in a feeling of calmness. As you 'centre' yourself and feel the connection of your feet with the ground, imagine, as the middle-ages mystics did, a line of energy running into your body from the depths of the earth. In this grounded position, have an image of the life-forces from the fire at the earth's centre through to its surface, filling your body and circling around your heart. Then shift your attention to the power and radiance of the sun and draw down its healing force through your head, into your body, to circle around your heart. From below and above you are filled with the universal energy of Being. The Holy Spirit who renews the face of the earth is now renewing your body, mind and soul like a new creation. As those two currents of life move within you, around your heart, they circulate like your blood does, and reach every part of your body. Then visualise them moving through your skin, shining out from you as God's grace, to encompass all those you love, all those who asked for your prayers, all those you are trying to love. Finally, extend your arms from your sides, at shoulder-height, and turn slowly through the four directions, tracing a circle of power, the Celtic *caim* of protection around you.

Be a living sacrifice of praise

DAY 11 The reflection and practice from yesterday is still in my mind and body. From the centre of the earth up through my feet, from the heart of the sky down through my head, from the light outside, and from my deepest soul within, I visualise God's energy flowing in and out. Every step I take, every breath I draw is a gesture of gratitude. My whole body becomes a small, living sacrament of praise and thanksgiving. I can feel my mind slowing down, my body relaxing, my breath growing even. I list everything around me as reasons for honouring my Lord – everything that is perceived by any of my senses, all my body members, the person I am, my family, the unbelievable richness of friendship and of the hearts that love me, the efforts being made to heal the broken minds and starving bodies around the world, the courage of those who have devoted their lives to the cause of peace.

To prepare for the new millennium I spent six autumn weeks with the Benedictine monks in Pluscarden, in the north of Scotland. In a hallowed thirteenth-century abbey, inhabited for life by a group of cheerful monks, a constant mantra of love is chanted for God's glory. Day and night, while the world is sleeping under the moon or turning around the sun, the song is always rising. As I listened to the cosmic sentiments of the psalms about the mysterious loveliness of the divine Artist, I felt we were created to praise. In gentle harmony and with great care, this ceaseless stream of blessing and deep affection arose with power on behalf of a terribly busy and distracted world. St Augustine said, 'Only the lover sings.' At Vespers on my first evening, for instance, we chanted in Gregorian style and in fulsome, rounded Latin, these lovely images:

If I flew to the point of sunrise,
or westward across the sea,
your hand would still be guiding me . . .
It was you who created my inmost self,
and put me together in my mother's womb;
for all these mysteries I thank you:
for the wonder of myself . . . (Ps 139)

The early morning Vigils and Lauds were gathering into one moment of pure praise all that every star and sea-shell, every fish and elephant, every city and desert, every heart – broken and healed – was offering up, in its own way, to the divine Parents of its life. There's something about praise that raises the spirits. Especially when it springs from a deep awareness of the love and meaning at the centre of our lives in general, and of each moment in particular. Praise and thanksgiving shift the focus of our attention from a self-indulgence with our own condition to a healthy attention to the Creator of the universes. In one of the weekday Eucharistic Prefaces we find, 'You have no need of our thanksgiving O God. Our prayer of praise adds nothing to your greatness, but it makes us grow . . .' Praising God honestly and truly from the heart, however, does not always come easily or naturally. I often have to pray my way into it. I number it among my *Breathers* because to praise and glorify God with as much of our attention as we can muster, we must first detach our mind from whatever has trapped it. And in the detachment, as I keep emphasising, is the way forward to wholeness.

All the *Breathers* presuppose this perennial key to springing the prison doors which lock us in – the ability to separate ourselves from what is overwhelming us at the time, to disentangle ourselves from the baited hook for which we fell. I cannot emphasise enough the importance of this exercise. It is like the opening 'gateway' movement before any of the *Breathers* are embarked upon. It is like the even, conscious breathing behind every ballet-movement or song or prayer. It is like finding and holding on to a rock as we tumble, out of control, down a waterfall, or, getting a foothold in a cave behind the waterfall and, released from its compelling power, watching it all happening, from the inside, so to speak. That moment of awareness when such a critical detachment and release happens in our conscious minds – that is when the goal is already within sight. I cannot think of a single self-help book, spiritual or psychological, that does not focus first on this initial distancing.

Here is an example of what I mean – a way of stopping being the victim of your negative thoughts, a way of establishing your independent, sufficient and free identity over against the deadly fascination of jealousy, envy, anger or fear. On a distracted morning, for instance, when I'm drawn to this particular

Breather, I begin by choosing to move my attention from those clamouring thoughts to positive perspectives by noticing, for instance, all the small miracles that I continually take for granted. I don't have to look far. They are crowding around me and within me. For a start, the sun has risen again. And better still, so have I. I am in the middle of this experience called life. It has its ups and downs, its joys and sorrows. But it is life. And I'm living it to the best of my ability. And it is marvellous and wonderful. There are people who really love me. There is a world that, in spite of all its wars and sins, is still a most beautiful place in which to live. And a whole new day, full of all kinds of possibilities, is waiting for me to live it and to love it. Already the focus of my attention has shifted and the first step into reshaping my mood and my day has begun. And already, too, this is the experience of grace, the work of the Holy Spirit, a taste of redemption, a glimpse of the abundant life. At this point, the liberating blessing of praise is calling our hearts and voices. The demons have gone – at least for a while.

Praxis 11

Once again you are gifted with a whole new day, twenty four priceless hours for you to fill as you will. Free of charge, and offered once only, they can be lived in a cul-de-sac of fear or against an infinite horizon. Let today be a day for reaching out in thanksgiving, a day of expansion for your heart, a day for breathing out of your system the suffocating baggage of yesterday's and yesteryear's left-over baggage. So reflect for a little while this morning on the power of blessing and praising that we all carry. Just as your heart and breath bless your body with life and energy, so too you can bless the world and its people with your love and compassion. Today, when you meditate, in the still centre of your being encircle in a halo of light, one by one (as you did with your 'enemies' a few days ago), all those you wish to bless, including your life-long friends, your recent friends and the people you will encounter at work and in your social life today. Look at their faces with a heart full of compassion. Let the powerful love of God vibrate outwards from your still self, bringing relief and joy to their lives. I know people who, as they walk along the street, drive their cars or ride on a bus, send out blessings on everybody and everything, with every breath and touch. The more powerful your attention to the meditation in the morning, the more sure will be the peace you spread throughout the day.

Have you the courage to be?

DAY 12 There have been times when I feel as though I'm driven into a corner, whimpering like a whipped dog. One thing after another, one person after another seems to plan for me another pathetic day. Now here comes *Breather* Twelve. When I'm given the grace, for an instant, to move outside my fear, to look at myself from beyond the reach of my anxiety or panic, I suddenly see how I have allowed myself to be victimised by all and sundry. I have handed over to others the responsibility for my own life. I have given permission to events and people to decide my moods and levels of misery. This drifting away from the anchor into unsafe waters can happen quite suddenly. I have forgotten my fine heritage – a proud cultural and religious tradition. When I begin to remember this and the divine powers of birth and baptism at my disposal, I feel a stirring deep within me. It is a glorious sensation – to realise oneself to be the inheritor of the gifts of creation and the graces of incarnation. It is the simple and unique moment of destiny, the time of turning. The running away stops and I face the enemy.

Now with an unholy greediness I open my being to the gift of courage. I storm heaven for it. With the cheek of an impatient child I demand it. A quiet power fills my soul. The courage to trust, to trust wildly and without caution, to take big risks, to become quite foolish and imprudent in my confidence in God, to stop being so damned careful all the time, to become the faith I profess. I try to incarnate my belief in the fifth gift of the Holy Spirit (fortitude) into my very psyche. This awakening to the presence of the Risen Christ within me is both an experience of death to my fear, and of new life to my inner power. It comes pouring in once I open the sluice gates of my being. It fills my body and soul in abundance. I pray for it to happen when death itself is around the corner. When we face up to death, I've heard it said, even in small ways, we are afraid no longer, because all fear, ultimately, is a fear of dying.

This *Breather* is pure gift. While the initial awareness of God's closeness provides, for the moment, the lift and spirit we need, it takes much longer to actually become the grace of fortitude.

Grace builds on nature and must shape itself into the contours of time and space. Down this road to freedom, there are many questions to be explored. Are we motivated by fear or love? Is fear to be fought against and banished or, like any other emotion, is it to be integrated and transcended? How do we feel the fear and do it anyway? Where and what is the gift in fear? But for now, the *Breather* brings a temporary relief. The cycle is broken by calling in, as Jesus did in the garden, the angels of God. We come from a long line of spiritual heroes and heroines – the 'cloud of witnesses', prophets and confessors, apostles and mystics.

To feel the fear, and then to face it, is to be empowered. It is as though the angels of light are waiting until the fundamental option is made, before pitching in behind the brave one. To be half-committed is not to be committed at all. Only when the boat is actually pushed out do the winds and the waves move in behind the traveller. There is another face of mystery here. Full and fearless commitment enlists the energies of all the positive forces, urging, drawing and inspiring the questing soul onwards. A little more of Goethe's spirit would do us all a power of good:

Whatever you can do
or dream you can, begin it.
Boldness has genius,
power and magic in it.

Among our ancestors were giants and champions, slayers of the dragons in the arena of courage and love. They faced the wild elements, they faced their wild enemies and they faced their own wild, inner selves. These are the women and men who remind us who we are, who are the wind beneath our wings, who light the furnace in our souls, who surround us gently when the chill fingers of fear close around our hearts. When thoughts, feelings and images such as these stir and then grow and thunder through my being, I quickly reclaim my lost ground and move on, all the stronger, into the mystery and mercy of God's strange ways.

Life of my life, I shall ever try to keep my body pure,
knowing that Your living touch is upon all my limbs.

I shall ever try to drive all evils away from my heart,
and keep my love in flower, knowing that You have
Your seat in the inmost shrine of my heart

It shall be my endeavour, today, to reveal You in my actions,
knowing it is Your power that gives me strength to act.[18]

Praxis 12

Before the chatter-box of your mind is switched on, find your usual quiet place and posture. Gently shut down the flow of thoughts, as you would dam a stream, so as to see more clearly the river-bed through the still water. (I'm always trying to let this happen! The Dalai Lama, who first offered this image, knew well the cost of achieving this simple goal.) Surrender yourself to God's dream for you. It is a dream of great strength. Trust that the grace of courage will fill your life from now on. Today, you face the fear in your life. You do not judge yourself for being frightened, or condemn yourself for being a coward. In your still soul, you invite into your depths the courage of God. Imagine a sailing ship helplessly drifting with the current, waiting for a breeze. And then it comes. A powerful wind crackles and fills the limp and lifeless sails. With heart-swelling pride and intent, it powers its way into the unknown oceans, scattering smaller craft in its majestic wake. And so with your soul. 'I can do all things in him who makes me strong.' (St Paul) Every morning I pray St Patrick's Breastplate with its words of power. 'I arise today through a mighty strength, the strength of the Trinity, of Christ's resurrection, of love, of nature, of God's strength ...' You will be aware of the change in your physical sensations, your pulse rate and your energy, when the surge of this grace of fortitude courses through your body and soul.

Lighten up

DAY 13 There are mornings when the left-over worries and unpleasant memories of yesterday's encounters are waiting at my bedside, to leap into my head and heart with their deadly whisperings, even though I had hoped they were lost in the night. It takes precious hours before I finally find the space to begin separating myself from the energy-draining cloud. I do this by asking to lighten up, to be more gentle with myself. I shake and lower my shoulders, take a few deep breaths and relax my face. Later on, if I find a chance for a quick walk in the country, I do a bit of a hop and a skip. Sometimes, while hopping and skipping, I emit sounds from my gut, to exorcise my anger or anxiety. It is at this point that, occasionally, out of sight on the other side of the hedge, when they hear or see me, sheep, cattle, pheasants and the occasional unsuspecting farmer relieving himself among the rushes, make a wild dash across the field for the safety of an outhouse or haystack. So I pray for the gift of humour, of not taking my life so seriously, of realising how little I can do to control or predict it. 'How do you make God laugh hilariously?' 'Tell her your plans for yourself!'

A friend who is sharing our inner journey here in Little Falls, was telling me about her training, a few years ago, for work with the Maryknoll missions. One session was about the most important quality a volunteer could have, when setting out for several years of overseas service. Some said, 'a special calling', others said holiness, patience, self-esteem, and so on. Nobody, except the veterans, gave the 'right' answer – a sense of humour. Was it Nietzsche who said that he might consider becoming a follower of Jesus, if Christians could manage to look redeemed? It is believed that a deep murmur of laughter was the most profound background to the creation of the world, and that God still wears a constant beatific smile when contemplating the world, even with all its misfortunes and horrific self-destruction.

A few days ago I was travelling to the Twin Cities with Peg, our counsellor, and found myself getting all hot and bothered about the finer points of our debate. Peg was discussing calmly; I was arguing heatedly, getting all tense and worked up.

Suddenly I said I was sorry and began to laugh. It just happened. But somewhere within me I must have noticed the utter point-lessness of losing my cool over nothing. Such a waste of precious energy that could have been invested in a more loving kind of talk. I was delighted with myself. So was Peg. She joined in, and we just let it out! The previous week at the Centre, a seminar had been devoted to the topic of 'Healing yourself with your own voice'. It was about finding liberation, release and empower-ment in the search for our personal and integrated sound and authentic voice.

Another example of being saved by laughter was during an interview, by Radio Belfast, about a recent, rather challenging book of mine called *Lost Soul? The Catholic Church Today*.[19] Towards the end of the allotted time, the interviewer's last ques-tion was, 'Father O'Leary, there may be bishops reading your book who would say that it is yourself, and not the church, that stands in danger of losing your soul. What do you say to that?' In an instant I felt the tension of fear and panic rising up within me. How should I answer? Would I defend myself vehemently? Just at the moment when I was beginning to relax and feel good about my performance up to then, things had taken a very un-expected turn. But the interviewer, a true professional, had spotted my guard going down and, with elegant timing, had thrust the poisoned spear home. So much can pass through your mind in the time it takes to draw a breath. Something incongruous about the whole moment struck me forcibly. I began to laugh, easily and genuinely. 'What's so funny, Father?' she asked. 'The bishops,' I replied, 'are probably right.'

When I reflect on these moments and others like them (I wish there were more), what strikes me with some pleasure is that they reveal a certain diminishing of my vain ego. It is said that you can tell the true teacher from the indoctrinator by their facial expression when a student disagrees, even aggressively. The genuine teacher will smile at this challenge in the mutual search for truth; the dogmatic one will either be taken aback momentar-ily, get angry, sneer loftily or sulk (inwardly) as I sometimes do, after Mass, when my homiletic efforts are not fully appreciated! The laugh brings a lightness and lift that is such a perfect de-fuser of tension, and of impending, useless conflict. It releases all kinds of stress-reducing, peace-inducing endorphins within us.

Another good friend of mine identifies the turning-point in

her long years of misery with her awareness of the absence of laughter in her life. She had forgotten how to laugh. From that time on, by challenging her cloud of loss and deep disappointment, she began to hold a different view of her serious situation, developing a more positive and confident attitude to what had seemed a rather hopeless scenario. In fact, by dwelling on the optimistic dimension of her most difficult life at that time, she began to see the disguised blessing within it, the gift within the shadow and, as a result, her character, her soul, were immensely enriched and strengthened, and still are.

There is an affinity between laughter and humility. People who can laugh at themselves, even in the most serious circumstances, are usually down-to-earth and very loveable. The Buddhists, and many of our own Christian mystics, have little doubt about the overall physical and psychic health and balance of energies that follow on a constant readiness for hearty laughing. This *Breather* is about becoming more aware of the power of laughing, especially at ourselves, in our lives, and to believe that whatever is bothering us today might benefit from, if not a huge belly-laugh, maybe a brave, spirited smile and a shrug of the shoulders.

Ah, the light dances, my Darling, at the
centre of my life; the light strikes, my Darling,
the chords of my love; the sky opens; the wind
runs wild; laughter passes over the earth.

Mirth spreads from leaf to leaf, my Darling,
and gladness without measure. The heaven's river
has drowned its banks, and the flood of joy is
abroad.[20]

Praxis 13

Light a candle today as you begin to pray. And, as a background for your meditation, play a little of your favourite music. Visualise your body as light and vibrant. Visualise it at play. As you breathe, evenly and consciously, remember your favourite way of playing as a child. Was it skipping on the spring roads, going barefoot in the summer streams, building snowmen in the magic of winter, kicking through the brown leaves at autumn time? How can you bring a little play into your life today? Maybe a hop and a skip, or a quick shout (if you find yourself in a place with no people) or a few quick swings, slides or bounces (if you happen to pass a children's playground). We really are dreadfully inhibited. We are terrified of doing something different. From where did this fear come? Never mind. You could go barefoot around the house more often than you do, or outside if the weather is fine. Sing a song from beginning to end, a little louder and with more gusto than normal. Trying to remember your childhood games is one thing; bringing your body into action with the memory of them is quite another. There is a healing and wholeness about this kind of re-connecting. Given complete freedom, someone said, the first thing we would all do is play! Create some simple, playful, even 'useless' activity every day. Break the mould of your Catholic work-ethic, of your childhood echoes of guilt, and dare to waste a little time today! Bring your prayer this morning, and every morning, to a respectful, deliberate end.

Can you let go of fear?

DAY 14

Fear ranks high as the most immobilising of human emotions. Many people see fear as a wall that closes in on them. As they approach the wall, fear increases and movement stops. They turn and retreat. Fear becomes a power of limitation. But it can also become a prelude to illumination. It can trigger bouts of endurance, fortitude and determination. Once we realise that fear is nothing but an obstacle to be scaled, it can be used to our advantage. Fear is subdued, first, with confrontation. Otherwise, like a shadow-sniper, flitting from tree to tree in the darkness of the forest, it totally impedes our journey and turns it into a hopeless retreat. As with the elusive sniper, it is not easy to identify the object of our fear, to see its face. Because of that there is no denying its extraordinary power. I see examples of this huge influence every day, in myself and others – times when we are afraid to say or do the loving thing, the compassionate thing, the truthful thing. Evil thrives, not when evil people do evil things, but when good people do or say nothing.

In fact, the process of doing this, of moving towards the void of fear, of breathing into it, is a huge part of the quest for the true self. As with anger, once we enlist and utilise the energy of fear in our own favour, we move along our path to wholeness with swifter feet. Each time you seek out the features of fear, you find a face behind the face, behind the face. Eventually you are led to the truth. It is as though the shadows of fear are the spaces into which true love has not yet entered. That is why perfect love casts out fear. And that brings the fine grace of courage to the soul. Eleanor Roosevelt said, 'You gain strength, courage and confidence by every experience in which you really stop to look fear in the face. You are able to say to yourself, "I lived through this horror. I can live through the next one, too." You must do the thing you think you cannot do.'

For some personality types, fear is a crippling reality. It can lead to a half-lived life. It strikes at the heart of the 'abundant life' that Jesus came to restore to us. He struggled himself with this particular demon, as well as with many others. Rarely does anyone sweat blood. It takes extraordinary terror for this to hap-

pen. 'Father, if it be possible, let this chalice pass from me ...'
Trust and faith are powerful antidotes to fear. Only God's grace
sends these forces surging through the body, mind and spirit.
Trust liberates where fear imprisons; trust empowers where fear
debilitates; trust affirms and enables where fear disheartens and
drains; trust resonates through the whole person, calling out
and drawing forth, where fear shrivels the spirit, destroying
confidence and killing the soul.

Since most of my own shadow stuff is about fear I often use
this *Breather* when the light grows faint. It grows faint at those
times when I hear, from somewhere deep inside me, those warning voices, from parents and neighbours and seminary sermons,
'Don't do it. Play safe. Hold tough. Be a sound man. It's too
risky. Be prudent. Don't be different. What if you fail?' *Breather*
Fourteen is about taking a deep breath and saying yes to life,
about believing in myself, about being aware of my anxiety and
fear yet still being authentic and integrated. It is the time for reminding myself of my guardian angels, those most wonderful
rays of God's protective light.

It is then that I hear another voice whispering in my soul as-
suring me of my infinite value and worth, of my preciousness in
God's eyes, of my immunity from being damaged or destroyed
beyond swift recovery. 'If you should find yourself in the valley
of darkness or walking across the barren desert or sense the
presence of the devil, no evil will you fear because I am there,
loving you into your hero-heart.' This is when I tell myself that I
can do and be all things in Christ. With God's grace I too can
work miracles. In trust I claim the self-confidence and power,
hard-won by Jesus in a terrible death, so that I can be free. The
quite unbelievable truth is that all I have to do is not to stop
God's awesome love from transforming me. I simply let it happen to me, flow through me, encompass me. It is only love that
transcends fear.

This *Breather* is not about fighting fear. The more we fight it
the more virulent it becomes. There will always be fear. It is not
destroyed by making wild lunges against it or sudden changes
to avoid it. Press it down and, like a cork in water, it only leaps
up again in a moment. Once we get rid of it at one location, it immediately attaches itself to another object or person. We can all
recall some of the unsuccessful ways that we tried to control or
eliminate fear. The most risky, potentially damaging and useless

'cure' is to turn, in panic, to some 'quick-fix' programme, guru, or particular relationship to get rid of fears regarding security, finances, loneliness, self-esteem or sexual inadequacy.

Our fears are compulsive and must be faced and integrated, not fought. By visualisation, affirmation and by grounding yourself through bodywork, you will find the light flowing in to the shadowy places of fear. Such delightful experiences may seem like miracles, and feel like heaven, but they are ours for the asking and for the taking. At great cost, these liberating graces were made readily available for us by our Saviour. Only fear stayed nailed to the cross. 'Fear not, for I have redeemed you. I have called you by your name. You are mine. When you take on the swirling rapids, you will not drown. When you walk through the leaping flames, you will not be burned. You are precious in my sight.' (Is 43)

In general, we perceive life coming to meet us either as gift or threat. Likewise, we are motivated, as a rule, either by love or fear. Our goal is to be always motivated by love. Our suppressed fear makes this so difficult to achieve. A first step is not to be afraid of fear or to resist it. Neither does it help to start blaming life or people for your condition. What helps is to enlist the rich energy of fear by turning it round to serve you. Face it, feel it, breathe into it and then gently press on with your life, your passion, your project or your relationship. Open to it in a vigilant and loving way and you will sense a shifting of the blockage within you. It is helpful to remember, too, that it is only the fearful folk, attempting this daunting adventure, who can be graced with the God-like quality of courage. Those with no fear can never be brave.

Praxis 14

Let today's meditation be a moment of thanksgiving for those who have loved you and who love you still. As you light the candle and listen to the music, hold them in your heart. With each deliberate breath, send them a blessing and a prayer of gratitude. The hearts and bodies that love you are the sources of the courage that empowers you to face your shadow, your sins and your terrors. They are the ones that make divine love tangible. Without people to hold us, the night is too dark, the forest too sinister and the journey too long and lonely. Try to embody your thankfulness as you breathe in and out. This is a high form of mutual empowerment, of graced presence to each other. The mystic Meister Eckhart preached that if the only prayer we ever said was 'thank you', it would be enough! Not one breath of love, not one heartbeat of gratitude will go to waste. And when you finish your meditation today, make a decision to call, or write, or send a present to those faithful friends who are loving you into your courage to face your fears, and to live, in each one of your days, the abundant life promised to us by Jesus. These people are, in fact, your angels – God's way of revealing to you the saving, liberating reality of what it means, in the first place, to be born into this world and then to be baptised into the Christian community.

Do you know how loved you are?

DAY 15 Self-hatred plays havoc with the quality of people's lives. We are told it is a very common condition, the reason for many desperate and expensive visits to counsellors and therapists. Mostly, this self-destructive force, together with its accompanying cohorts of loss of self-esteem, anger and depression, began in childhood. And those negative voices are on mental tapes that play fast and furious with sickening and deadly consequences. Nor are they easily erased. Those tapes are reinforced by the current oppressive voices and systems, religious and political, that amplify our doubts and guilty feelings in our adult life. Every time we let ourselves be victimised by real or imagined rejection or ridicule, we are feeding our tendency to self-hate. To encounter these tendencies, dismantle them and use them positively is a lifetime's work.

Yet, amazingly, miracles do happen! *Breather* Fifteen is about building up an unshakeable belief in one's own God-like self. This happens for me when I reflect on how important I am to God, how unconditionally I'm loved, how delighted God is to watch me. Ronald Rolheiser offers us a picture of God that never fails to move me. A mother is looking out through a window, standing behind a chair, waiting for her daughter and son to get off the school bus at the bottom of the drive. The little girl comes first, her fair hair, unribboned, flying free, her laces undone, her books slipping from under her arm. Trying to race her to the front door, the boy's tie is awry, his socks around his ankles, his shirt sticking out. There are two reasons why the mother leans forward on the chair-back. She needs to keep them both in view for as along as possible; something tells her she mustn't miss this moment. But also, she needs the support of the chair because her knees are trembling and her body is growing weak from the sheer waves of utter love that are contracting her heart.

Few of us have experienced unconditional love. Within the human context, there is always some kind of price to pay. Rightly or wrongly we feel we must earn or merit the love of others. It is no easy art, to do the loving thing. The profound poet Rainer Maria Rilke was well aware of this truth.

For one human being to love another human being:
that is perhaps
the most difficult task that has been entrusted to us,
the ultimate task, the final test and proof,
the work for which all work is merely preparation.

Loving God and loving another have much in common. 'The love with which God loves us,' preached St Augustine, 'is the same love with which we love one another.' He also insisted in his well-known, pithy phrase *noverim me, noverim te*, that our knowledge and love of ourselves was a dimension of our knowledge and love of God. Because of the distrust and fear that grips our anxious hearts, as we reflected upon in yesterday's *Breather*, we rarely surrender to true love. Older Catholics, especially, tend to haggle and bargain through their prayers, penances and good deeds, so as to demand, deserve or barter for divine forgiveness, unconditional acceptance and ultimate salvation. It takes a special grace to undo the fear-filled damage to our bodies and souls arising from the instilled anxiety, in childhood, about judgement and punishment.

The point of this *Breather* is that this special grace of unconditional love is always available to us, always freely offered by the God who is so in love with us. The grateful acceptance of this reality changes everything. It is something like what happens when we fall in love – only more so. God's crazy infatuation with us, we can never lose. All we have to do is to believe in it. And just as the new falling of this winter's persistent snow is covering, in waves and shades of beautiful whiteness, the entire bleak countryside around Little Falls, a tiny, rural city crafted around this frozen bend of the Mississippi, so too the ceaseless falling of God's ecstatic desire for us will transform our often-barren hearts, souls and bodies – our very lives – into unimaginable power and beauty. And we need images and symbols to help us understand the mystery of God's love for us. Incarnation's revelation is a song to be sung, a poem to be recited, a new language to be 'learned by heart'.

It is very important to understand that love is another fundamental means of cognition and a 'language' in its own right. Thus did Pascal enunciate his famous motto, 'the heart has reasons that reason does not understand' and insist that one must distinguish between the *esprit de geometrie* (objective, measurable, knowledge of the head) and the *esprit de finesse*

(heart-language and heart-thinking) . . . which can bring us to
the beating heart of reality, to the tabernacle of our being, the
Inner Christ.[21]

Once we draw near to that 'beating heart of reality, to the
tabernacle of our being, the Inner Christ', then our tendencies to
judge and condemn, to worry about past hurts and future disasters, begin to loosen their grasp on us. Because fear and guilt
cannot co-exist with love we become a new creation. We reflect
and shine with the light of God in whom we live and move and
have our very being. We grow beautiful before ourselves and
others. And the good news of *Breather* Fifteen is that this 'little'
miracle often happens quite suddenly.

Praxis 15

Let every intake of breath in your prayer today be a welcome to the unconditional love of God. Try to feel, in your body, the sensation of divine loving and delight. As you breathe out, give back that compassion to the whole world. Regularly and quietly, let the awareness of being held and nurtured by the arms and heart of God, become stronger and more vibrant in your very bones and muscles, in your eyes and face. You may struggle with this exercise; you may doubt its truth or wonder about its efficacy. But these temptations are to be gently set aside. We are assured by Jesus of God's unwavering and life-giving devotion to each one of us. Also, during the course of the day, create regular 'trigger moments' to be mindful of the constant embrace of our Tremendous Lover. When I was small, everyone stopped what they were doing in our house when the clock struck the hour, or in the fields when the angelus rang. When the Buddhist 'mindfulness bell' pealed out, everyone would pause for the length of three mindful breaths, before continuing with their work. These 'mindfulness moments' for you might be occasions such as leaving the house, when returning home, before eating the evening meal, on awakening or simply before going to sleep. Just a mindful pause, three breaths, an awareness of angels.

Look out! Beyond here be dragons

DAY 16 The theologian and philosopher Pascal once said that wars would cease if occasionally men *(sic)* could only sit quietly alone in their rooms. Even though the wisdom of the ages offers inner silence as the necessary doorway to peace of soul, there are not many takers. It is too risky. Yet it is the task of Everyman. The Search for Self, the Grail Quest, the Hero's Journey are all archetypal adventures imprinted in the human psyche through these and many other universal and national legends, folklore and myths of the human race. The journey takes us outside our conscious knowledge and learned behaviour. This is a dangerous and forbidding place. When the cartographers of the medieval atlases reached the end of known territories, they would add some ominous words on the edge of the map: 'Beyond here be dragons.'

However, for some people, and maybe for you, since you have persevered thus far, it is a journey you must take. After many decades, I am still trying to travel that journey, sometimes excitedly, often very frustratedly. I am often drawn to practice one simple yet profound exercise. *Breather* Sixteen is about becoming more conscious of my breathing. I collect and draw in my thoughts, hanging like rags on every bush of yesterday, blown by every expected change of wind tomorrow, and try to find that still place at the centre. At times, in spite of lurking dragons, it blesses me like balm. As I breathe in and out and pause between breaths, I approach that place where breath meets non-breath, where life meets non-life, by sense-awareness first, as the rhythm of my heart-beat changes. Then, whether with a mantra or some kind of simple symbol, the crossing is made into the unexplored emptiness of the spirit. This is a refined version of our daily meditation practices which become a window into the real mind, our true essence.

Stopping thinking, the Dalai Lama says, is like stopping the flow of a stream so as to see both the water and the river-bed startlingly clearly. (I haven't reached that stage yet!) Anthony de Mello says it is not about doing anything, or thinking positively, or trying, or searching, or desiring. Our breath is the universal life-force that sustains all things and unblocks whatever threatens the flow of life. We simply become more aware of its rhythm and pace, and follow where it leads us. When our daily dose of potentially negative experiences comes upon us, this *Breather* reminds us to breathe deeply into the blocked emotions or numbed-out feelings that we carry, mostly unknowingly, somewhere deep within us.

I don't pretend to be sure-footed around all of these issues. When it comes to understanding incarnate mystery, we are all novices. As we surrender to the Spirit of love, we know that we are called to a harmony of mind, body and spirit. We simply try to bring our thinking, our feeling, our breathing and our physical sensations together. Neither do I want it to sound too easy. I'm just reflecting with you about things I get glimpses of. The healing power of the breath, for instance, if we trust it, will find and stabilise our imbalances and unblock our energy. Also, as I wrote in the Introduction, some form of bodywork is nearly always a huge help in bringing integration and wholeness. Because the body remembers every hurt and abuse, because it holds in its muscles, tissues and bones, every buried and bitter emotion, it is only through the anointing and sacred touching of our bodies that such pent-up tears and fears can be released.

All I can say is that when I'm there or thereabouts in my attempts at meditation, hovering over the way my breath comes in and goes out, aware of the pauses and spaces in-between, I believe it is the most important, most fertile, most blessed experience to have. As well as the witness of the holiest women and men of every century since humanity evolved, another part of my reason for believing this stems from the classic scriptural, doctrinal and devotional definitions of God as 'pure essence', 'pure being', 'source of life'. Beyond thoughts and feelings, beyond bodily sensations and psychic visions, the act of breathing and the beating of our hearts must be the nearest we get to 'pure being', to the 'source of life'. The author of *The Cloud of Unknowing* wrote, 'If you look at God in the perspective of eternity, there is no name you can give him, nor is there any experience or understanding which is more fitting than that which is contained in the blind and lovely beholding of the word *is*.'

I simply believe that when I'm floundering around in there where my body senses things and where I consciously focus on my lungs filling and emptying, I'm very close to the 'origin of existence', to God. Even though no words are said, no prayers are formulated, no images entertained and often, only blank, black nothingness prevails, I still believe that it is the most loving, healing, redeeming and growing place to be. It won't always feel like that. In fact it is a form of what in classical theology is called the *via negativa*, the way of unknowing – a belief that darkness and emptiness are the safest and most secure definitions of God. It takes practice, patience and blind faith to persevere in such unfamiliar places.

It is around this territory of destiny that we find, at the boundaries, the notices we have already come across earlier on our journey so far – beyond here be dragons. When this happens it does not mean that we have lost our way. More likely it means that we are nearing a threshold and that our proud ego is in panic. It was at the time of his final decision to surrender all to God, that the devils of temptations struck so intensely at the spirit of Jesus. And he was in turmoil. With so much at stake, his ego, his false self, his inner demon, waged a final and violent battle. It is the moment of truth. By that I mean that when, in our own uncertain spiritual journey, we round what looks like just another bend in the road and there, confronting us with frightening power, is a drove of dragons, it is only then we can be sure that we are approaching God.

Praxis 16

This morning, or this evening, settle yourself for meditation in
the usual way, by paying attention to the sensations in the different parts of your body. There is no better way to regain your
peaceful centre than by doing this. Whatever the source of your
unease, the focusing on the body in your meditation is the most
powerful antidote to your distress. It is a safe and grounded
place to meet your dragons. Remember, too, that there is a sense
in which you are your own dragon. Now move to your breathing, as you have been practising, keeping in mind the intimacy
with God in so doing – as we reflected upon in today's *Breather*.
Stay with each breath, one full breath in, one full breath out,
keeping your heart and mind open and free. It is the trying that
counts. Then focus on your heart and its beating. Just by shifting
your attention to its rhythmic pulsing, you will notice and feel
its gentle power. Finally, sense the extraordinary ebb and flow
of the blood to all the extremities of your body, moving out,
drawing back in the most amazing way. This is a tall order, even
for those who are ready. As well as circulating health and energy
all through you, visualise the stream of grace and blessings that
are flowing into every crevice of your soul. Stay with this and let
yourself be overwhelmed by the wonder of the miracle that you
are.

Transform the negative cycle

DAY 17 How do I transform the negative experiences of life into light and energy? How do I reconcile and redeem what is sinful and hurtful? How do I become an alchemist, changing the dull lead of my days into pure and shining gold? I'm asking these questions on Maundy Thursday. *Breather* Seventeen transcends all the others. (See also *Breather* Thirty One and *Praxis* Thirty One.) It is the life-work of those who yearn to be 'other Christs' by sacrificing their egos completely, taking on themselves the 'mind of Christ'. Raised up with our Lord on the cross, they purify and draw all things to God. The theory and practice of *Breather* Seventeen are both crucifying and exhilarating. To be a reconciler is to be one who fully lives out the dying and rising mystery of Good Friday and Easter Sunday.

When I succeed in being a reconciler, instead of reacting to, resisting or reflecting back the negative emotions and attitudes of those around me, whether in a one-to-one, communal or wider context, I take into myself the jealousies, cynicism, bitterness and hurting of the people and the systems of my community. Like a re-cycler, a holy incinerator, a reconciler, I filter, through my redeemed essence, I transform, in my very own self, like Jesus did, the sins into graces, the curses into blessings, the destructive forces into life-enhancing gifts. We're at the heart of the matter here. So often, when someone hurts us, all we do, either in self-justifying anger, forced politeness, self-righteous correcting or condescending 'forgiveness' is to add force to the negative vibrations, by turning them round and re-directing them in an even more deliberatively negative way, back the way they came. Richard Rohr writes about our destructive habits of denial and projection.

> If the small ego is not transformed, the negative emotions (hate and fear) will be either denied or projected elsewhere. The process of both denying and projecting is called 'scapegoating', from the Jewish ritual of putting your faults on a goat that was whipped out into the desert. The object of our wrath, like the poor 'escaping' goat, is completely arbitrary and artificial. It has nothing to do with truth or reason. It has

to do with fear. Then a plausible and much-needed projection screen will always be found for our little drama. The amazing thing is how well it works. We rather easily displace our fears (and negative emotions) on to other people, other issues, other places, other times. Anything rather than bearing the burden myself. Only the true self can carry such anxiety, such ambiguity, such essential insecurity. It is much too much for the false self to carry. If our pain is not transformed through union with God, it will always be transmitted to others. You can take that as an absolute.[22]

It takes a big soul to avoid complicity in the scapegoating which is happening in churches and in states today, to unite the suffering of our lives with the passion of Jesus, to burn out its own and others' evil in the ego-less emptiness of its own holy space. I'm sure that this is what Zen teaching means by 'the big mind' and what Thomas Aquinas meant when he described the greatest virtue (as we have already seen) as that of magnanimity, a largeness of heart, big enough to be always forgiving and understanding. This is what brings light into the world. But those who hate the light will attack it. The attack is always subtle, sudden and deadly. Yet, this is where the malignant energy is contained and neutralised. The attack backfires. In his *The Road Less Travelled*, Scott Peck wrote, 'It was evil that raised Christ to the cross, thereby enabling us to see him from afar.' (p 279) The same author, in his *People of the Lie*, quotes an old battle-scarred priest who said, 'There are dozens of ways to deal with evil and several ways to conquer it. All of them are facets of the truth that the only ultimate way to conquer evil is to let it be smothered within a willing, loving human being. When it is absorbed there, like blood on the sponge or a spear into one's heart, it loses its power and goes no further'. (p 269)

This is slow and risky work. Sometimes all I can do is smile at the mess I make of this lofty option. But I've reached a point now of not taking myself too seriously, of knowing there's no such thing as getting it right always in this life, of not letting my constant failures and sometimes doubtful motives, stop me from forever continuing to try. At the end of the day, this *Breather* is about compassion; it is only compassion that will enable us to transform the negative cycle. We live in a desperately destructive world, where evil is perpetrated under the guise of nationalism and religion. It is hard to be a reconciler. But we have no option.

There is only a world to weep over, only victimisers who are themselves victims, only a larger evil in which I am complicit and often profiting from. Only the mystics and the sinners seem to be able to see this. There is no one to blame, accuse, or punish. There is only the holding of it all, the bearing of the dark mystery of human sin and failure, until our patient love and our suffering of it break through to resurrection. There is no redemptive violence; there is only redemptive suffering.[23]

In his *Conjectures of a Guilty Bystander*, Thomas Merton writes of a time when his understanding of Christianity was becoming truly catholic, and when he realised what the cost for him would be in trying to bring this about. As it was with Christ the reconciler, so it would be with Thomas. 'If I can unite in myself,' he emphasised, 'the thought and the devotion of Eastern and Western Christendom, the Greek and Latin Fathers, the Russians with the Spanish mystics, I can prepare in myself the reunion of divided Christians . . . We must contain all divided worlds in ourselves and transcend them in Christ.' (p 21)

All of this is uniquely the work of God. As we have just seen, to take on the forces of evil is a dangerous business. Only fools rush in. The wisdom of the churches insists on the real destructive power of bad spirits. Only experienced ministers, for instance, who have prayed and fasted and are well prepared with the crucifix, the prayers and holy water, are deemed suitable for those strange encounters with the devil. That is why, also, I think it is important to point out that sometimes we are well advised not to ingest the poison of certain people who are around us daily, especially if we are feeling vulnerable. There is a time not to be a reconciler. Some bad food is too deadly for our spiritual stomachs to digest and transform into good energy. There are toxic people whom we do well to avoid until we are stronger. There is an evil that most of us cannot handle. And if we don't transform it, we'll transmit it. There is great need for discernment here. God will find another way. Even Jesus himself was very wary of the extreme evil concentrated in a number of possessed victims. He also instructed his disciples to shake the dust of certain places and people from their feet and to get out of town pretty smartly. You cannot force the river. Neither can God force the grace of salvation and freedom on any creature.

May I end, with two lovely attempts at enabling us to look at our own shadows and negative attitudes with compassion, and even gratitude! I begin with our friend, Rumi:

This human being is a guest-house;
every morning a new arrival;
a joy, a depression, a meanness –
some momentary awareness comes
as an unexpected visitor.
Welcome and entertain them all!
Even if they're a crowd of sorrows,
who violently sweep your house
empty of all your furniture;
still treat each guest honourably.
He may be clearing you out for some new delight.
The dark thought, the shame, the malice –
meet them at the door laughing,
and invite them in.
Be grateful for whoever comes,
because each has been sent
as a guide from beyond.

The second is from the teachings of Bearwatcher, an Apachi medicine man:

In the Apachi language there is no word for 'guilt'.
There is no word for 'shame'.
Our lives are like diamonds.
When we are born we are pure and uncut.
Each thing that happens to us in our lives
teaches us how to reflect the light in the world;
each experience gives us a new cut, a new facet in our diamond.
How brilliantly do those diamonds sparkle whose facets are many,
to whom life has given many cuts!
So when you feel that the rain is no longer playful but harsh,
and when the snow has lost its beauty,
hold your diamond in your hand.
Do not feel shame. Do not feel guilt.
Think instead of the way you may now reflect the light of the world,
and be thankful for the new cut
you have received on your diamond.

Praxis 17

Today's meditation is about 'blessing ourselves', a phrase familiar
to all Catholics, so as to be ready to continue on our demanding
journey and to travel light. The Sign of the Cross is a most powerful ritual. Slowly trace the symbol that is stronger than death or
evil across your mind, body and heart. In the Christian tradition,
you are placing yourself under the protection of the Blessed
Trinity, of the Creator and Sustainer of Life, of the Saviour of
Humanity, of the Spirit of Love. Bless yourself a few times, deliberately, prayerfully and courageously. As you touch your
forehead and chest, in the Eastern tradition you are opening the
brow and heart *chakras* of vision and compassion. According to
Jewish esoteric practice, as you touch your left and right shoulders, you are activating the spiritual centres of mercy *(chesed)*
and strength *(geburah)*. In the myths of history, the warrior put
on the magic shield of invisible security. A few days ago we reflected on the recitation of St Patrick's Breastplate to begin the
new day. These mornings, as I awake, I make the Sign of the
Cross with a sense of power and destiny that I never had before.
Having pondered on the mystery and wonder of how the un-
armed light-carrier can burn more brightly, even in the absorbing of the shadow-evil of others, Scott Peck ends one of his
books with this observation: 'Whenever this happens there is a
slight shift in the balance of power in the world.'

Trust that all is harvest

DAY 18

A fairly common cause for our more sombre moods often springs from regrets about lost opportunities, about decades wasted on trivial pursuits or energy whittled away during careless years, with nothing to show for them, no trace of anything lasting. Whether we now see ourselves as victims of either workaholism or laziness, few escape the often-searing regrets and bitter feelings about what is, with hindsight, perceived as futility or pointlessness. Those wasted years, those crazy choices, those costly mistakes, all that useless effort! Either way, especially during certain decades of our lives, most of us are prone to reflect, at some level of intensity, about how much we have achieved at both a professional and personal level. Such emotions and memories have an awful deadness reflected in energy-less bodies, empty faces and spiritless souls.

At meditation today at The Spiritual Centre, our Director played some Gregorian chant as an introduction to our prayer. Even though I'm now in the seventh decade of my present incarnation, I was swept back, in an instant, to the chapel in All Hallows College, Dublin where, all decked out in our surplices and soutanes, many young men of twenty were singing the *Kyrie* at Mass. Later, as I sit here in my little room, in the State of 10,000 lakes, watching the bleak sun casting a cold shadow on the unrelenting snow outside, I begin to cry. Oh where did they go, my bright dreams and green vision? What has happened to the fresh innocence and high hopes of young Donal? After 45 years of restless struggle, broken promises and repeated beginnings, I'm still unable to master even the primer in holiness that I'm now re-reading (Caussade's little classic *Self-Abandonment to Divine Providence*) which I first studied in 1955.

The last few times, before today, that I cried, was when leaving someplace or some friends yet again, with a sense of anger and self-pity at my perennial wandering, never settling down, never feeling at home, always unfulfilled and incomplete. It last happened as I set out on this pilgrimage from Yorkshire to the Mid-West of the USA, in search of something I can't name, packing my bits and pieces into bags, leaving some of the most

wonderful, loving, forgiving and exciting people that I have
ever met, and fighting back the tears. Because this is a pattern of
my life, it is important how I explain it to myself. I can see it as a
feckless, careless refusal to be constant, responsible and reliable
or I can see it as a searching for a love that includes but transcends all other loves. In the paradoxical flow of life and of my
own changing sub-personalities, sometimes it appears to be one,
sometimes the other.

Endemic to every human heart is a spark of infinity, a hint of
the divine, a small mystic who has designs on eternity. In some,
this spark has almost gone out; in others it burns with a fierce intensity that carries a permanent ache. The more attuned to beauty
we become, the more the longing increases. The late Cardinal
Basil Hume, in his 1999 De Lubac lecture, quoted George
Herbert's poem *The Pulley God,* which explains the necessary
place of 'restlessness' in the human heart. The only gift withheld
from creatures is that of 'the comfort of rest':

> For if I should, said He,
> bestow this jewel also on my creature,
> he would adore my gifts instead of me,
> and rest in Nature, not the God of Nature:
> so both should losers be.

> Yet let him keep all else,
> But keep them with repining restlessness;
> Let him be rich and weary, that at least,
> If goodness lead him not, yet weariness
> May toss him to my breast.

My heart goes out to folk who are in despair at the perceived
failure of their lives. I think it is a desperately sad thing to happen to anybody. I want to hold them close and fill them with
hope; to tell them of the wonder of their lives; how they have, all
unknowingly, changed the world; how, one day, the love they
have incarnated in the hearts of others will be their shining
selves in heaven forever. *Breather* Eighteen flows like balm over
the tormented soul. This is how I understand it. Through the incarnation of God into human form, everything, except deliberately chosen lovelessness, is sanctified. There is nothing that is
not saved, no blade of grass without God's signature; nothing
that is neutral, valueless or bad. Julian of Norwich called this
'the doctrine of universalism'. When Jesus descended into hell,
even sin was redeemed and made potentially redemptive.

Darkness is no longer threatening; death no longer has real power; nothing goes waste; to live, to breathe, to be, to have a heart that beats, is already to be pulsing with divine energy; all is harvest. The Buddhists would say it a little differently: it is the way it is; and the way it is, is perfect; and one day that truth will be revealed to you.

Such are the blessed revelations I whisper to myself in the dry times. There is nothing the baby does that is not delightful to the parents. Whether playing, sleeping, dribbling, on the potty, sucking a nipple, a thumb or a toe, there is beautiful meaning for the adoring mother. So with us and God. Even the most ordinary and routine actions and duties of our roles in life, may be the most sacred of all. The mystery of God is experienced as paradox. The Holy Spirit spins gold from the bare threads of our threadbare days. Antonio Machado wrote 'I dreamt last night, oh marvellous error, that there were honeybees in my heart, making honey out of my old failures.'

And so, there it was before me, early on a morning of unsuspected spiritual depths and richness, in our little prayer-room, this lovely reflection from the Indian poet Tagore, brought by one of my seven angels:

On many an idle day I have grieved over
lost time, but it is never lost, O God. You have
taken every moment of my life in Your own hands.

Hidden in the heart of things, You are
nourishing seeds into sprouts, buds into blossoms,
and ripening flowers into fruitfulness.

I was tired and sleeping on my idle bed and
imagined all work had ceased. In the morning
I awoke, and found my garden full with wonders of flowers. [24]

Praxis 18

Yesterday we blessed ourselves, on the head, heart and shoulders, with the Sign of the Cross. Today we touch ourselves again, believing in the healing and anointing power that we all carry by virtue of our humanity and of our Christianity. Jesus was always touching people. Each morning I place my cupped hands over my eyes, the thumbs on either side of my nose, for a short while, and then over my ears. I believe in the wholesome energy that I carry as a child of God. I then place my hands on my neck, and, over my clothes, on my shoulders, on my throat, on my heart, across my ribs, on my lower stomach and on my bare feet. I breathe easily. It only takes a few minutes. While I'm doing this, I pray for the unblocking within me of the channels of physical and emotional energy. I do it mindfully, prayerfully and gently. We carry so much of the health and healing that we need, in our own bodies. The prayerful anointing that I'm suggesting is invigorating for both body and soul. And so, at meditation today, maybe you could enter into the possibility of a deep transcendence in your way of looking at the mystery of life, and at who you think you are within it. Place your hands on your body as I have described. Do it with total conviction. End your prayer with an act of trust in God's dream for you – the abundant life, the emerging beauty of your hidden self, the carefreeness of the birds of the air.

Create a bit of heaven on earth

DAY 19

Sooner or later, no matter which approach we take towards having a healthy mind in a healthy body, no matter how many self-help books we read or processes we undertake, no matter how many prayers we say or pilgrimages we make, our inner work will never be complete without the experience of forgiving and of being forgiven. Without these experiences, there can be no true, inner peace or freedom. Heaven is on earth when forgiveness happens. Without the words 'I'm sorry' and 'I forgive you', the promises and vows of love ring very hollow indeed. The need for a constant openness to forgiveness comes, you will have noticed, like a refrain, throughout these *Breathers*.

We cannot take any short-cuts or detours to avoid the reality of forgiveness. It is a profound spiritual power. There is no alternative. The reason is this: whatever the nature of the negative emotions from which we suffer and from which we crave some release and healing, we are essentially acting out of a sense of hurting, a basic pain. And where there's hurting, there's anger. And anger held on to, becomes resentment and even hatred, taking a huge toll on our emotional and physical health. The royal road to psychic balance, mental stability and even bodily well-being, passes through forgiveness.

Breather Nineteen is about briefly reminding ourselves of the miraculous power of reconciliation, and of never giving up on trying to practise it. The reasons for perseverance in this quest are many. How can any of us, for instance, be in a fit state to bring the liberating good news of equality and fairness to anybody else, near or afar, if we ourselves are still crippled and de-humanised by gnawing antipathy and resentful mind? A sound tree produces good fruit. Writer and broadcaster Gerard Hughes SJ said, 'The inner and outer are one. My effectiveness in justice and peace work will depend on my readiness to face, acknowledge and be reconciled, as far as possible, with those who have wronged me, or whom I have wronged. This does not require heroic acts of will on my part, but trust in the power of God's Spirit at work in me.'

Maybe we can only accept the grace when we are ready for it; maybe we have to be partially destroyed by the evil within us

before we can transcend it; maybe we really do not want to let go
of our resentment at all, for a variety of reasons, and this is very
common. I feel worlds colliding when I hear the last bitter words
from people on their death-beds about prohibiting a family
member, or former friend, from coming to the funeral. The only
reason that I offer the amazing grace of forgiveness as the sub-
ject-matter for this *Breather* is because of its central place, its
heavenly power and the immediate results, in restoring us to a
lovely and unimaginable peace of mind.

Earlier this morning, as millions of tiny but unique
snowflakes, delicate as gossamer, decorated all the space between the Minnesota earth and sky, our group here at the
Spiritual Centre was enabled, in a variety of ways, to enter
deeply into the fragile world of our hurts, whether we were the
victims or the perpetrators. Apart at all from purely mandatory
religious considerations such as the commandment to forgive
each other, we explored the experiential, therapeutic reasons for
beginning the long process of offering or accepting forgiveness,
whether to do with ourselves, others or God. I say 'a long process'
because, very often, there are many stages in arriving at forgiveness. It does not happen all at once, as in 'going to confession'. It
is more like the stages of bereavement. And I also mention the
'forgiveness of self' because this is usually the most difficult part
of the process.

We are still the victims of those who hurt us, as long as we
keep our hearts closed to them. They are still a threat to us, we
still fear them, and this brings only tension and anxiety to our
already stressed-out lives. As long as we are blaming someone
by clinging to old anger we continue to block out the light from
our souls. Ask yourself whether this is true for you, just now.
We will never have peace unless we keep our anger 'current'.
Like every new negative emotion, anger lasts but for a very
short while, before either leaving us completely or deteriorating
into something dangerous and poisonous. It latches on to some
life-pattern from the past, assuming another identity. It therefore destroys our own self-esteem. So we begin to despise ourselves. We cannot hate someone else and love ourselves any
more than we can hate ourselves and love someone else. This, I
think, has something to do with the rather terrifying gospel
admonition that if we don't try to live out the blessing called
forgiveness, then, even God cannot forgive us. (You may wish to

interpret that famous passage in Matthew's gospel in a less blunt
way.)

There is something important I want to say, as I finish this
reflection about forgiveness, whether it be the forgiveness of
others, or, as we have just considered, what is almost always
more difficult, the forgiveness of ourselves. I'm not sure if I can
put it well. It has to do with understanding forgiveness, not as
repeated acts, out of duty or for eternal reward, whether seven
times or seventy times seven. It is about becoming and being a
forgiving person all of the time. It is about being permanently
wrapped in the grace of compassionate awareness of others, in
general, or of another human being in particular, in whom war
is being waged between the forces of light and darkness; of understanding the precariousness and fragility of sanity and of the
infinite and bewildering complexity of the human spirit. It is
about the hundred hidden pressures and temptations of certain
souls and of the power of their passions, of the utter vulnerability
and brittleness of broken hearts and bodies and of the confusion
of unprepared minds when faced with powerful and deadly
attractions. It is about the unspeakable sufferings and cruel
harshness inflicted on beautiful and sensitive psyches both in
childhood and in later life, and of the innate propensity of certain
temperaments, more than others, to be seduced by false allurements. It is only those familiar with the ambiguity of their own
strange contradictions and paradoxes of inner and outer behaviour, who are safe sacraments of divine forgiveness. Such people
will never judge and condemn. Their self-aware hearts are too
wise. 'To know all,' wrote Saint Antoine Exupery, as he realised
with shocking clarity in the despair of the desert, 'is to forgive
all.' Such are the times when we allow the rainbows of heaven to
break through the mists of earth.

The day before Bishop David's visit to our parish, a few of us
were clearing up around the church. As we came upon a patch
of green and growing things, Tony, with his hoe at the ready,
asked me 'Are these weeds or flowers?' The question set me
thinking. In case you're still waiting, Tony, two years later, this
poem, *Quilt*, is my answer!

As they say it does,
just before I died, like a small ocean
my life flattened itself into a wavy
patch-work quilt.

Just before they went glassy, as they say they do,
my eyes could suddenly see everything clearly
and at the moment of the last stitch,
they understood the whole complex interweaving.

It was such a revelation that my last
breath was filled with wonder.
Because nothing was as I had been told.
Everything, in fact, was the other way round.

My darkest times were now the brightest patches
and the 'sinful' pieces held them all together.
The weakest patterns came from my proudest moments,
and my deeds of goodness were the most threadbare of all.

The finest colours, it was revealed to me,
were mixed at night, without permission.
And the shapes of beauty, only now so fitting,
were drawn with my left hand – wild and pagan.

And then I saw a shy and shining thread of gold –
(and remembered telling it in confession)
– a moment that was unknowingly divine.
It was then I saw the beckoning angel.

So now stand up, the fool with power
to say, 'it's a weed' or 'no, 'tis a flower'?

Praxis 19

Begin, today, with a decision to forgive from your heart the person who has hurt you most or is now hurting you deeply. So often, as with the initial step in overcoming an addiction, it is a matter of one full-blooded and grace-inspired decision, in God's name, to let go. People are daily destroying the quality of their own living and of those around them, by a hard and harsh clinging to past wounds. You have probably been thinking and praying about this for some time. What remains is the whole-hearted decision to begin something unbelievably liberating and new. Maybe today is your day to turn the key on your own prison door and walk out, no longer a victim of the past, but a free person. You have suffered enough; your heart and mind and body have been drained, for too long, of their precious energy by the poison of resentment which closes us to grace. The lungs of your soul are gasping for the fresh air of forgiveness and letting go. Today could indeed be the first day of the rest of your now abundant life. With these quiet but deep reflections, bring your meditation to an end. Try to keep something of this conscious resolution near to your thoughts throughout the day.

Send for reinforcements

DAY 20 When we were children, having been beaten in a fight, or if the odds seemed too great, we would call on, or threaten the opposition with our fathers. (In actual fact, I have seen nobody to put the fear of God into even the biggest of bullies as the impassioned mother!) In all walks of life, both in professional and personal affairs, we look for help, we send for reinforcements, we call up the reserves. Even Jesus, in his final and most intense crisis, was well aware of the legions of angels waiting for his signal. *Breather* Twenty is about our guardian angels. Do you remember our sometimes perfunctory morning commitment to our invisible and holy minder? We were probably closer to them then than now.

Angel of God, my guardian dear,
To whom God's love commits me here,
Ever this day, be at my side,
To teach and guard, to rule and guide.

Almost everyone will have had a mysterious, unexplained occurrence in the course of life. The lucky escapes, however, the unexplained little miracles, the sudden rescue against all the odds and a hundred other unusual moments that most people write off as coincidences or fortunate chance, others thank their angels for. Dismissed with the rosary, benediction and Gregorian chant, we are now witnessing a rather shamefaced reclaiming of these gifts and so many other lost graces since the Vatican Council of the sixties. Guardian Angels were among the casualties. But now they are well and truly restored.

As many people are becoming more comfortable with an increasingly spiritual and mystical dimension to life, accepting the possibilities of holy presences everywhere (as the old and new Catholic catechisms of the faith assure us), there is an immense belief springing up in the old teaching of a divinely-designated angel, appointed to take care of each one of us, all our lives long. Her task is to guard and guide us, to advise and warn us, to anticipate the dangers in our path. Sometimes we may have more than one. A very wise man in Dublin once told me that I had seven. One of them is the guardian angel of all my relationships (who is, incidentally, severely overworked!)

This *Breather* is about the divine and delightful spiritual guide at our disposal every minute of the day. It is about pausing for a brief chat, a moment to ask for help, maybe to scream for it, a turning aside in private intimacy, as one might do with a tried and trusted friend. Our spiritual self has a natural affinity with angels. Many searchers are finding a new voice with which to address their heavenly companions. As with our dreams, our angels wait to be called in and called up. They will then lead us to the Holy One in the sanctuary of our souls. In this place, the external anxieties and confusions of our lives are seen in their true colours and in perspective. They become manageable.

There is a whole, beautiful world within and around the one we live in. The time and place environment we daily inhabit is, if we could but truly see, teeming with a life of energy and with astonishing beings of compassion. Do not be afraid to think in this way, to imagine such a space within and around you, and to live in it. We are surrounded by cynics who ridicule this kind of imagery and conviction. Because they often speak with the voice of ecclesiastical 'clout' or medical authority, they keep many needy ones from exploring, and being nurtured by, the very powerful resources and storehouses of nourishment provided for them by a compassionate Parent. Such dismissive critics are often only acting out of their own ignorance, fears and poverty of imagination.

Along with the words of the Deer's Cry (already mentioned above and also known as St Patrick's Breastplate) where the 'mighty strength of the love, obedience and service of the Cherubim, angels and archangels' is invoked at the beginning of each new day, I love to remember this verse, by John Bate, whenever I'm frightened:

You feel that dangers hold you tight;
remember, nature guards you well.
The way you are is shield all right
from horrors heaped up out of sight.
Be sure that nature guards you well;
trembling within, without so bright,
don't doubt there was a saving spell
cast at your birth for your delight;
your very nature guards you well.[25]

With typical brevity, Shunryu Suzuki, in his book *Zen Mind, Beginner's Mind*, about Right Attitude in Zen meditation, writes,

'The point we emphasise is strong confidence in our original nature'. This confidence in original blessing is not always obvious in the emphases of other religions and of most Christian denominations. In *Sitting by the Well*, Marion Woodman teaches that 'We are moving into a new paradigm, leaving the old structures behind. Where do we go for guidance? I suggest to you that we have no place but our own well. We all have this well inside. We must drink or die.'

Praxis 20

As you begin your meditation today, reflect on your belief in a protective presence around you at all times. Having settled yourself into prayer in the usual way, in body, mind and heart, ask yourself whether you believe that an angel, however you may wish to understand that word just now, is always near you, anticipating, preventing, persuading, so as to keep you safe and well. Your angel is the presence of divine providence taking an extraordinary interest in promoting your general well-being and your most secret and intimate joy. It is yourself that will benefit psychologically and physically from a delighted acknowledgement of her presence and from a regular conversation, as happens between two intimate friends. Remember that this beautiful belief is not a New Age discovery; it is as old, at least, as Christianity. Most people still resist believing in their guardian angel. Exactly the same as they struggle to believe that God loves them unconditionally. As you leave your prayer-place today, try to remember to call on your angel the moment that you are in sudden need – the car won't start and you're already late for work or late for dropping off the kids at school, or you get a flat tyre, or you can't find a parking space, or you feel a panic-attack coming on, or the boss wants to see you, or your child is late coming home from school. Miracles do happen – because your angels are around.

Become what you love

DAY 21

I'm sure that God loves people who are consumed by a passion for the possible. So many of our negative moods, 'bad hair' days, lifeless morning feelings come because we are unaware that our possibilities are limitless. St Paul reminds us that we have already received what we ask for, if we do so with any bit of conviction; that we can do all things in Christ who makes us strong. The only boundaries to our horizons are those we draw ourselves. We compromise in our feeble prayers as though God did not really love us unconditionally and as though God wasn't really all that powerful. We half-heartedly and piously settle for less. There is no 'fire in our bellies' to make us shout at God. Instead of storming heaven like privileged warrior-children of the almighty Lover, we hang around behind the shadows, wondering if the Lord of the castle is in a good mood.

Maybe we are right to be afraid. Some prayers, like the Our Father for instance, are downright dangerous. Maybe in our heart of hearts, when we pray for 'God's will to be done unto us', we know that we will be transformed all right, but crucified first. And there aren't many willing sacrificial victims around these days. *Breather* Twenty One is about nurturing within us the utter certainty that whatever we ask for we will receive. And we will receive it abundantly, extravagantly, pressed down and running over. Louis Mumford wrote that one day we will live in the castles we dream of. Only believe it and all that your heart longs for is already yours. A transfiguration can happen and we begin to radiate a new beauty.

So pause for a moment, take a deep breath, and visualise the place of glory promised by God to those of transparent hearts and translucent souls. This is promised for our lives now, when the beauty of the 'hidden self' is revealed for all to see, when 'the abundant life' is what we live every day. This *Breather* is about daring to be different; daring to dream the impossible dream because it is not impossible at all, since it is ours by birthright. It is about taking Jesus at his word, about breaking through into a whole new way of seeing everything, of understanding what Thomas Merton meant when he shouted, 'Make way for Christ whose smile, like lightning, sets free the song of everlasting glory that now sleeps in your paper flesh, like dynamite.'

We are called by the gods to grow into what we know, to incarnate our wisdom, to become in our bodies all that we love. We physically enflesh the insights of our divine hearts, even as we do so with the body and blood of Jesus. We work out our vision in the raw material of the lived fragments of each day and night. We incorporate, in full roundedness, in complete knowing, in embodied wisdom, the beauty that is God. 'Because I made you, I will wed you', we read in Isaiah, 'you are my delight.' The Sufi poet, Rumi, offers this advice:

Whatever it is you wish to marry,
go absorb yourself in that beloved,
assume its shape and qualities.
If you wish for the light, prepare yourself
to receive it; if you wish to be far from God,
nourish your ego and drive yourself away.
If you wish to find a way out of this ruined prison,
don't turn your head away from the Beloved,
but bow in worship and draw near.[26]

Our bodies are possessed by Spirit. We fall in love with her. This possession does not mean a distancing from the material world we live in. But it does mean that our perception of it is entirely transformed. The shadows of our fallenness are no longer seen as the triumph of evil but as the raw material of the experience of true resurrection.

What may appear as a loss, for instance, in the material world, is seen differently in the world of Spirit, where nothing can be lost. This does not mean that our grief just disappears; for our losses remain. The sorrows of life embitter some and shatter others. Yet these same sorrows may set all of life against the backdrop of eternity and become a fountain of refreshment, a living energy to draw on. The agony of Jesus, the pain of Mary, and the submission of Muhammad are reminders that suffering cannot be avoided – and yet we are blessed ... People and events do not lose their significance; they become witnesses and evidence of spirit, transparent to its radiance. We begin to see the qualities of the Creator in the creation.[27]

Like a heap of feathers in the path of a raging tornado, like an ice-cream in the blazing sun, when we open our hearts and bod-

ies and minds to the love and meaning in the soul of the universe
and in the soul of God, nothing can prevent the transformation
and transfiguration happening. What we love, what we adore,
we become.

Once embarked on the journey of my soul, abroad to others
and at home to God, I keep reminding myself to give it my all, to
travel the course at full tilt, to experience it right to the hilt. This
Breather Twenty One is about the passion, urgency, risk and
commitment that spring from a powerful love. Maybe that
sounds like an excessive drive in a path of self-nurturing and
gentle persuasion. But is there really a contradiction in both approaches? Did not the One who commended to us the carefree
and effortless existence of the birds of the air and the lilies of the
field, also say something about the dreadful fate of the luke-
warm and the truth that heaven surrenders itself only to those
who take it, intensely, by storm? Evelyn Underhill, a wonderful
student and traveller of the spiritual path wrote:

> We know a thing only by uniting with it; by assimilating
> with it; by an interpenetration of it and ourselves. It gives
> itself to us, just in so far as we give ourselves to it, and it is
> because our outflow towards things is usually so perfunctory
> and so languid, that our comprehension of things is so per-
> functory and languid too. Wisdom is the fruit of communion.
> ... Because he has surrendered himself to it, united with it, the
> patriot knows his country, the artist knows the subject of his
> art, the lover his beloved, the saint his God, in a manner which
> is inconceivable as well as unattainable by the looker-on.
>
> (We said) that mysticism was the art of union with
> Reality; that it was, above all else, a science of love. Hence,
> the condition to which it looks forward and towards, to
> which the soul of the contemplative has been stretching out,
> is a condition of 'being', not of 'seeing'. . . growing and
> stretching into more perfect harmony with the Eternal One,
> until at last, like the blessed ones of Dante's vision, the clear-
> ness of his flame responds to the unspeakable radiance of the
> Enkindling Light.[28]

A disciple returned to his guru, after many years of long
preparation for his hoped-for enlightenment. 'Have you learned
how to be consumed by the passion of Love?' he was asked. The
disciple modestly held up his hands. His fingers were burning.
'Come back,' said the guru, 'when your whole body has become
the fire.'

Praxis 21

When it comes to authenticity, you cannot do better than mix with children. They are at one with themselves. They are the love that drives and draws them. During your meditation today, let the presence of children – your own or others – flow into your awareness. They do not doubt their parents' love. They radiate with it; that is the energy that makes them shine. But first settle yourself down to an inner stillness. Notice your joints relaxing, your shoulders dropping, your face softening. Now quietly turn your attention to those children you know and enjoy. Think of them at play, smiling or crying, always true to themselves. Recall their total commitment to the matter in hand, their effortless and spontaneous movements, their complete lack of self-consciousness. They carry an immense healing power because they are still undivided in body, mind and spirit. It is little wonder that Jesus so often held children up as the ideal to be honoured, if we are ever to understand anything about God or get to heaven ourselves. Is it possible to spend some (extra) time with (your) children today? Their hidden grace will soothe and heal your distress and worry. And don't just watch them. Join in the fun and go with their flow. It is good for us because, to our adult ways of thinking, it is purposeless. But we have all grown too serious. Close your prayer today with a plea to God about the exploitation and destruction of childhood innocence all over the world.

Know your heart-power

DAY 22

After many years of trying to be a more spiritual, rounded, human person I still flounder around in my petty reactions, negative traits and regular bouts of sulks and geri▲tric tantrums. To be honest, they don't bother me now as much as they did, mainly because I am much more adept at springing their traps and slipping their nets than I was before. I no longer simmer, stew or boil all day, a victim of my own blocked, self-destructive emotions. *Breather* Twenty Two is about unblocking our vibrant energies and balancing them, so that the power of our hearts can be released.

Like good violins, harps or radios, there are people whose spirits are fine-tuned to the voices, the graces, the vibrations, the music of other people and of life. Like the membrane in the leaf, they can hold it all together in right relationship and in due proportion. By shifting, holding, adjusting, trusting, like the falcon or hawk at high noon, riding effortlessly and perfectly on rising currents of air, they seem to be part of everything and everything a part of them. This centred stillness, this inner groundedness is something we can all aspire to. For a monkey-mind like mine, with its grasshopper attention-span, it may take a little longer, but I have no doubt whatever that it is the birthright and baptism-right of every one of us if we but want it enough. This *Breather* is to encourage us to pursue that possibility.

There is a story about the Rainman. Because of unremitting drought, the population of a small country at the edge of the world, was being decimated. For years there was no harvest because constant, scorching sunshine had made a desert of the fields. Nothing could grow. The babies were dying. Only a few healthy people remained. Then they heard about the Rainman. He could make the rain fall. They fed and prayed with the only two healthy youngsters in the land and sent them to find the miracle-worker.

After years they found him. He came, looked, listened, wept and disappeared into the hard hills. Forty days later the rains came. The fields went from brown to yellow to green. The crops grew, the animals played, the babies smiled. It was a season of joy, a nation of jubilee, a celebrating community. One evening an old woman remembered the Rainman. Where was he? Did nobody thank him? What was his amazing secret? Down in the valleys they found him. He smiled at their good news. No, he had no special secret or magic to offer them in case the drought returned. He had simply waited alone until he found and experienced an intimacy with his own true self. He had entered into his deepest spirit in order to be radically authentic. When the rhythm of his soul was even, the rains came.

The previous *Breather* was about setting the scene for entering this point of stillness. There is a sense in which the incarnation could be called the Feast of Balance (but not the balance between two dualistic polarities, which has nothing to do with growing or healing). It is, rather, the moment of perfect holding between time and eternity, history and destiny, body and spirit, humanity and God. It is not fixed and static. It is full of flowing – releasing and returning, imbalance followed by balance. It is the 'yes' of creation to the invitation of its creator. At such a moment in our lives, too, everything is possible. Just as the beating of the tiny heart of the baby Jesus set the tempo for the dance of the cosmos, so too must ours, if universal peace and justice are ever to prevail. One of Teilhard de Chardin's visions was about the way the planets turned and danced to the rhythm of one silent soul in meditation. And it is happening everywhere and all around us, but in another dimension of life, too close for us to see, and which cannot be measured or recorded.

Every time the compassion in our hearts can absorb the distortions of the human condition around us, salvation happens. Whenever our holy instinct for universal fairness swallows up our innate selfishness, the miracles of Jesus become as common as the air we breathe. To be true to ourselves and to others is to be true to God. When I am at one in my body, mind and spirit, creation, too, is at one. When the channels are open, the power surges through. Let the soul of one person in some attic burn with enough passion, and soon the whole city will be on fire. When the heart within is pure, the face of the earth reflects the light of heaven. Unbound, our souls are full of God's truth and compassionate power. According to Zen wisdom, our eyes, unblinkered, will unerringly see the true beauty of all things. Unblocked, our ears will hear the perfect music of creation. Christian mysticism holds that our hearts, pure and enlightened, can transform the earth.

One day, in the ancient times of Tara, King Lugaid the Just
was called to resolve a powerful disagreement between two
rival factions. After long debate the whole assembly waited
for their ruler to pronounce in favour of where justice obviously lay. When justice was pronounced, Cormac, a young
friend of the monarch, shouted out in horror that the king's
judgement was a false one. At that moment, one whole side
of the actual house – the side of it where the lie was told – fell
down the cliff-side. From then on, the year that followed
under Lugaid's reign brought disaster after disaster. No
grass came through the earth. No leaf grew on any tree. The
harvest failed. Nature was out of true balance.

It was then that the people recalled the wisdom of the old
women, the crones, that nature responds to our moral state.
The 'fír flathemon', the king's justice, brings peace for the
people and fertility to the earth. The king's wickedness
brings a reign of destruction. They retold the ancient lore:
It is through the justice of the ruler that abundances of the
    woods' treefruit are tasted;
It is through the justice of the ruler that milk-yields of great
    cattle are maintained;
It is through the justice of the ruler that there is abundance of
    high, full corn;
It is through the justice of the ruler that abundance of fish
    swim in the rivers. . .

I like to think that each one of us, when we act out of our true
essence rather than out of our false ego, when we refuse to betray our authentic self, when we are in close touch with our own
sacred centre in spite of persistent temptation, persuasion and
compulsion to conform and compromise – that when we act in
this way we transform every room we enter, every conversation
in which we take part, every relationship we engage in and
every project we initiate or join.

Praxis 22

Try the following guided meditation today if you feel a bit
'under the weather'. Put on some soothing music. Become aware
of the rhythm of your breathing. Then enter into the spirit of this
imagery. You are walking on wet, swampy ground. It is a
stormy day. You are laden with baggage – two heavy suitcases
in your hands, bags on your back – and you are struggling
against the wind and rain. You are feeling weak and sweaty and
very anxious. You feel yourself sinking in the mud and you try
to remain upright by grasping at the branches of a wildly sway-
ing tree. The flooding water is rising now, up to your knees,
pushing hard against you and you are losing your balance. You
are full of panic. The water is getting higher and the wind is
blowing a gale. The swirling, muddy water is up to your waist.
The threshing branch is whipped from your grasp. Your belong-
ings are swept away – bags, suitcases, clothes, shoes. You
scream as you collapse … Then you hear a whisper, 'Let them
go. You do not need them. You have but one life to save.
Surrender to God's power.' Suddenly you feel light and buoyant,
free and flowing, firmly and lovingly supported as you float on
your back in a still, calm lake. The sun is warm on your face.
Because you are deeply at peace, everything seems so different.
The miracle is that everything *is* different .

Celebrate your age

DAY 23

'Heavens, how you've aged!' exclaimed the Master after speaking with a boyhood friend.

'One cannot help growing old, can one?' said the friend.

'No, one cannot', agreed the Master, 'but one must avoid becoming aged.'[29]

Around mid-life many people get a little depressed about the meaninglessness of their existence, the futility of their achievements, the emptiness of it all. This reality, ridiculed by some, resisted or denied by most, can be an intensely difficult time of turmoil for others. It takes more than a *Breather* to reclaim the lost peace of soul during these particular decades. However, today I wish to mention a few thoughts about ageing in general and the kind of fairly common distress that it can bring. As I myself moved from my fifties into my sixties, I felt the need to sum up the directions of my life, to gather together the strands of it, to shed the fat of it, to try to simplify and refine it. 'What is the essence of my life?' I asked myself. 'To what am I devoting my best energies? For what have I a passion? What are the new opportunities thrown up by my journey through the decades? Out of the whole landscape, which is the bright field with my treasure in it?'

Even though there is no guarantee that increasing age brings increasing contentment, nevertheless, undoubted graces become available as we advance in years. It seems so sad that apparently the majority of people find their last decades filled with unhappy memories, unfulfilled dreams, and feelings of bitterness over the unfairness of life. During those few difficult years when I had to engage in the classic struggle with the condition of ageing, fighting off the fact that I was no longer young, denying my mortality, no longer agile in body or mind, *Breather* Twenty Three was an enormous help. I began to focus on the emerging sense of freedom that felt like a huge relief after a life of striving to succeed, always trying to please everyone, feeling guilty about taking time off, competing in often unconscious ways, and carrying a vague sense of anxiety about not being good enough at my work. Being somewhat ambitious by nature, I gradually became more aware of the victim I had let myself become, of the straitjacket that so restricted my true aspirations, of the cage that made it impossible for me to fly.

In an earlier book, *Creative Crisis*, I wrote about the fear and doubt that grip the heart at some time during the middle-years, that is between thirty-five and fifty-five. It is a moment of much anguish but of greater opportunity. For those who trust the timing of things, the stages of growing, the wisdom of the heart, there will be a call, an attraction toward a kind of compassionate presence and giving, that up to now has not been experienced. It is an ultimate evolution in the classic dimensions of growth and of faith, when a pure form of altruism and community-care, without the expectation of reward, take over the body and soul. There is something passive and submissive about the current striving for 'early retirement'. Samuel Beckett was in his nineties when he said something like 'Retire? How could I retire, what with the fire in me now?' Every decade of life, especially the later ones, brings whole new fields to be furrowed and ploughed, with seeds to be set, and harvests to be gathered. These are the decades of permission to try out ideas and projects that we dared not do at an earlier age, a time to give our creative imagination a free run with its passion for the possible. Around the so-called retirement decades, we should have the expectation for exciting new doors and windows to swing open, not slam shut; for previously unreachable horizons to seem attainable after all. Like the long-jumper on the run-up to the take-off board, to risk living right up to the moment of death is the surest way of having an impetus for the final leap!

The second half of life is not really a continuation of the first. I'm sure it was Carl Jung who claimed that what supported us in the morning of our earthly sojourn will not be sufficient to see us through its afternoon; and also, that the questions raised during those rich second-half decades are all spiritual ones. This *Breather* is to remind us about the profound spiritual re-shaping that ideally goes on within us at this sensitive time. The self-image is low, during these years of being stuck in a rut, because the new horizon is as yet unclear, with new priorities, new values and new goals to be identified. The original vision of childhood has yet to be recovered and then fulfilled. There are strains and tensions now because the beliefs and ambitions of the past do not sustain us anymore. This brings a sense of loss and maybe of anger too. There is a need to grieve for the passing of that season of life, as old perspectives give way to new ones. What drove us relentlessly up to now, no longer gives us energy. That is why it is called a crisis. But as we know, a crisis is the necessary context for a breakthrough opportunity.

Joan Chittister reminds us that as we watch time run out in one sense, we are released, in another sense, to live with a new intensity. She emphasises a quality of presence to others and to the world that may not have been possible before. The rat-race, the deadlines, the frantic trying to keep up with, or stay ahead of, the opposition, are over. Time changes the tempo. We begin to discern a different drummer.

> Then age modulates life. We cease to plunge headlong into every option, every event, glutting ourselves with all the savouries of life, unassimilated and untested ... Slowness becomes a virtue. We learn to live again, one activity at a time: this fine sunset, that fine egg, this symphony, that night on a fishing pier. Slowing down is the beginning of life. The fear of death gives way to the headiness of life ... In the second half of life everything we ever accumulated begins to disappear. We empty the cupboards. We strip and clear and bear the hollows of our tiny worlds till there is nothing left but the self, the memories, the footsteps of our lives. We find ourselves stripped of titles and offices and importance. Feeling empty and vulnerable, we are cast adrift to contemplate what we have become and what we have done for others. Then, just when it seems that nothing is right, we wake up one morning to our leaner, truer selves. We are, we discover, now offered the prospect of doing the really important things we may have been too important to do before now.[30]

For those who are trying to keep in tune with themselves, body, mind and spirit, and thus in tune with God and with others, there is a transcending and unifying spirituality in the gift of years. Ideally, it is a fertile time for the mystic in each one to grow and flourish. The immanence of God, the mystery in all of creation, the oneness of everything, the presence of eternity in the now – all of these begin to assume a more understandable and almost tangible reality. We undertake to enter the centre of ourselves where the love and meaning at the heart of the universe is revealed. If we keep our hearts open, these special years grow a beautiful harvest.

Then wisdom supersedes knowledge and life supersedes living. It is a glorious time of life, full of a richer kind of excitement but fraught with danger – because some people, still lost in time and speed, in things and the ego, can lose a sense of vision, crumble and quit. No longer young, they have no love of age. They crawl down inside themselves and wait to die, angry at the thought of it, full of despair and regret. But the truly spiritual person strides to the top of the mountain of life, looks down at the plains below, and laughs. There is no more climbing to do now. There is only the glory of the view.[31]

And that view is within us. It was always within us. It is, in fact, the wounded, child of wonder we have always carried, whose healing voice we have rarely acknowledged. I love thinking about *The Bright Field* by R. S. Thomas:

I have seen the sun break through
to illuminate a small field
for a while, and gone my way
and forgotten it. But that was the pearl
of great price, the one field that had
the treasure in it. I realise now
that I must give all that I have
to possess it. Life is not hurrying

on to a receding future, nor hankering after
an imagined past. It is the turning
aside like Moses to the miracle
of the lit bush, to a brightness
that seemed as transitory as your youth
once, but is the eternity that awaits you.[32]

I write as though all of this were somehow predictable and fairly easy. It is not. I struggle every day to believe all that I hold about these issues of love and meaning, faith and letting go. Some days I feel a real sense of doubt and failure; other days I am utterly convinced of the sheer magic of the revealed mysteries. I believe Lord; help my unbelief.

Praxis 23

Put on some gentle music. After preparing your body, mind and spirit in the usual way, become conscious of your breathing and let your thoughts drift towards scenes, shapes and colours of nature. Bring before you an image of your favourite country place. Lose yourself in it. Together with children and animals, to be in the presence of nature is both restful and healing. Do you have any opportunity today to walk in a park, to stand on a river-bank or cross a bridge over a stream, to look at the sky either this morning, this evening or tonight, and to wonder at the immensity and beauty of our wider home? If you feel drawn to a flower, a rock in the stream, a piece of wood, do not miss the message. Honour the moment and listen to the secrets of what-ever has caught and called your attention. And there is some-thing so special about the silence of it all. It is the creature within you, who is born and grows in the womb of this silence, who will be your beautiful and faithful companion during the most intense, vibrant and exciting stretches of your journey home. As you finish your meditation today, thank God for the birth and growth of this inner awareness which is already, in spite of the occasional doubt or negative reaction, transforming your life.

Listen to your inner child

DAY 24 There is, within each of us, a wounded child of wonder whose original vision is, unknowingly, our guiding light, not only in this world but, amazingly, in the next as well. You may not be familiar with the imagery and language about the inner child, a contemporary spiritual/psychological approach to healing and wholeness. The hurt and damaged child of our childhood needs to be picked up and nurtured at some time during the decades of our lives. Usually it is only when something traumatic happens that the adult will perceive the need to look within, and begin a new and nourishing relationship with the small but powerful presence we call your 'child'.

Breather Twenty Four is about listening to the voice of our divine child whose eternal heart is the continual link between the birth, death and after-life of our bodies and souls. By this I mean that the small baby carries fresh echoes of God within its tiny heart, and these are nearly always lost or stolen in the course of the span of our years on earth. This reflection is about the eternal importance of recovering an intimacy with that child because she is the unique doorway to our intimacy with God, and she is also that part of us which will live on forever in heaven. In this life then, so much of our health and healing has to do with recovering and developing a conscious relationship with our 'lost' child. 'Unless you become as little children,' Jesus insists, 'you cannot enter the kingdom of God.' There is an eternal quality about childhood. Childhood is not lived through, and then shed, like a skin or cradle that has served its purpose.

A child grows as a tree grows, wasting nothing, ever more itself as the seasons circle round it, realising its true nature and expressing that nature forever. The child does not gradually develop adulthood. There is simply an unfolding of what is already there. The fullness endures from the beginning; it is not acquired by stages. We do not lose childhood. Rather, at some point in our lives, and maybe for you that time is now, we rediscover that wounded and usually neglected child; we name it and greet it; we honour and affirm it; we ask its forgiveness. I repeat; it is our child, our very essence, who will lead us to the abundant life promised by Jesus, not just in this life but into heaven too.

Even though all of this approach and imagery may be quite unfamiliar and difficult for many, yet it is a most beautiful notion to be thinking about, full of mystery. The child within will reward us well for the time we take to understand, and then to listen. What a miracle in your life this *Breather* could work if you reflect on its revelation. Far from being a new-fangled notion, it is part of the wisdom of the earth; it is at the centre of our Christian worship. The baby at baptism is called the temple of the Holy Spirit, a priestess and a princess. One of our best theologians puts it this way:

> . . . we only become the children we were because we gather up time – and in this, our childhood too – into our eternity . . . we do not move away from childhood in any definitive sense, but rather more towards the eternity of this childhood, to its definite and enduring validity in God's sight . . . it is important in itself also, as a stage of man's personal history in which that takes place which can only take place in childhood itself, a field which bears fair flowers and ripe fruits such as can grow in this field and in no other, and which will themselves be carried into the storehouses of eternity.[33]

I'm always moved when I read these words. They are among the most beautiful I know. Please reread them because their meaning is not immediately obvious. They are such a splendid celebration of the uniqueness of childhood. At a time when the world is guilty of the most awful treatment of children, either through widespread child slave-labour, coercive military service, physical, mental and emotional abuse at home and in homes, they shine with truth. They reveal that, because God was fully present in the child Jesus, no less than in the miracle-working, crucified adult on the cross, God is fully present in every child as well, baptised or not. The Word of God was incarnated fully and perfectly in the child as child, just as in the adult as adult. These insights have often been best preserved by the poets rather than by the churchmen. In *It is a Beauteous Evening*, for instance, William Wordsworth reveals that he is no stranger to the presence of divine mystery in childhood:

> Dear child; dear girl! That walkest with me here,
> If thou appear untouched by solemn thought,
> Thy nature is not therefore less divine:

Thou liest in Abraham's bosom all the year,
And worship at the Temple's inner shrine,
God being with thee when we knew it not.

Today's reflection is to remind you that the qualities of child-hood, not of childishness, are alive and well within you, and you need to reclaim and celebrate them. Your true inner child is not ego-driven; your child is drawn by wonder, by play, by trust and, above all, by openness. These are the characteristics that Jesus was alluding to; they are the qualities that the best of our psychologists, too, encourage us to nourish in our hearts. Otherwise we will stray, tragically, from our true path of bliss. Small children somehow know that they have nothing of them-selves on which to base any claim to gift or favour, yet they still believe that love will reach out and enfold them. Devoid of adult pretentiousness, and full of their belief in being unconditionally loved, they have not yet begun the endless, competitive quest for self-justification, for proving their worthiness, for being in 'the state of grace', for relentlessly producing something better than anybody else. Here lies the freedom and joy of the daugh-ters and sons of God. The eternal child at play in the presence of the Spirit, teaches the Christian to say:

... we shall be happy because we shall be open-hearted and open-handed, for we shall know, in the depths of our hearts, that what we are and have is not ours but God's, and shall be glad to know it; we shall be happy with all the new-found gaiety of the child re-born within us, the child who has everything to enjoy and love and nothing to lose; we shall be happy because we shall know that we are no longer in the darkness, that spring has replaced the spirit's winter, the 'rains are over and gone', and that if we are faithful, we live, not only now, but for ever and ever, in the Light that is life everlasting.[34]

Praxis 24

Today's prayer-time seems like a good occasion to recognise the presence of the wounded and graced child within you. You will need all your angels around you now, peace in your heart, a relaxed body and a quiet mind. There is a seriously damaged part of you that yearns for health and wholeness. Speak, today, to this damaged little creature. Give her a name – maybe the pet-name your family had for you when you were a child. There is no need to be embarrassed or self-conscious when doing this. Men who work out of their left brain (as opposed to their right brain which inspires the intuitive, imaginative and feminine) find this a daunting thing to do. You are addressing your most intimate self. Find a photograph of yourself when you were about seven or eight. Put it in a prominent place in your room. Address it. You don't have to say everything at once – maybe an initial acknowledgement of the presence of your lonely, neglected child, together with an apology for that neglect. Today's grace, for you, is about beginning a healing conversation of immense transforming power. (Do not be put off by your negative inner and outer voices that hold you back and make you doubt.) Please remember that deep and turbulent emotions are often released during this encounter. In a spirit of humility, self-forgiveness and discovery, draw your meditation to a close.

Be a child of the universe

There are mornings when the world seems to be closing in on me. Either I'm giving myself a hard time, or other people are. There is a big temptation to go back to bed. But most of us cannot do that. Many people have similar stories. They talk about days when life crowds too closely all around them. There is no personal space to breathe. The feeling is of being in a cramped enclosure. There is a sense of being threatened and trapped. Those of us who are somewhat claustrophobic suffer even more, both emotionally and physically. At a time like this we are overwhelmed by our powerlessness, our energy is usually low and our self esteem at zero. With our backs to the wall, it is not a pleasant place to be. Yet, the spark is not gone out; there is enough breath for one, last effort. It is at this point, I believe, that we have a choice.

On the one hand, I can submit to the negative forces. I can allow myself to be controlled by the enormous pressure and consequent fear and then panic, to the point of becoming almost immobile. I can hand over responsibility for my life to the perceived aggressors and, feeling beaten to the ropes, throw in the towel. I have seen people do this. They move back from the front line of life. They retreat to a small, dark place of temporary relief. Their hope and courage have gone. They have ways of justifying their sad escape. In reality, they have simply lost heart. None of us are strangers to these temptations, when our emotional and spiritual energies burn low.

But there is another way – the way up and out, for distressed and desperate souls. This way is about stopping the futile struggling and surrendering to the Higher Power. It is not about submission to outside pressure, but by opening up to the Spirit we carry within us. Deep in everyone is a wounded, eternal Child of Love. In *Breather* Twenty Four we became more acquainted with our inner child. Now we commit ourselves wholly to her presence within us. We call on her; we pray to her; we embrace her. She is our angel of light, our sacrament of God's extravagant power. At those awful moments when we feel the end is near, when we stagger with our baggage from lamp-post to lamp-post, this angel of comfort, touches the sleeping giant within us. And like a lighthouse in a stormy sea, like the resting Jesus in the windswept boat, that young heart of strength restores the harmony to our tormented lives.

I fill myself every day with thoughts, feelings and sentiments about my Child of Love, in every possible way. Otherwise, the negative forces from within and without, bring me rumours of doubts, anxieties and cynicism. All she tells, in spite of her pain, is the story of love. Only love can transcend fear and death. *Breather* Twenty Five is about the second option when we are cornered, at the end of our rope of hope, stuck in one of those desperate moments of our lives. It is then that we turn to the voice within, the voice that whispers, again and again, not to lose heart, not to despair, to take a deep breath and one more step, to reach out a trembling hand, somehow believing that it will be taken.

The good news is that we are already twice-blessed in our extraordinary capacity to love. By virtue both of creation and incarnation, we are potentially tremendous lovers. Because God, from the beginning, has concentrated the divine energy into our hearts to be released, like time-capsules of love, throughout our lives, and because Jesus made sure, at great cost, that we would never forget that amazing truth, these hearts of ours are dynamos of healing power. This grace is now the conscious dimension of our very being. Telling our hearts to love is like telling the wind to blow or the river to flow. Unerring and unceasing, our heart-child sings to us, especially in the twilight of our regular confusions or in the midnight of our utter, dry despair, the secret song of the morning, of the new beginning, of the trickle of fresh water, growing into a silent stream in the desert of our lives.

The late, beloved Cardinal Hume, in his last de Lubac lecture (1999), told us about one of the most moving accounts of the 'infinite glory' of love he had ever heard of. It was an incident from the life of Viktor Frankl, who was imprisoned at Auschwitz. Viktor's wife was also a prisoner of war at a neighbouring camp, but they were not allowed to see each other. There was an unique moment in his own life at that terrible place. He was stumbling to work in the icy wind before dawn, one of the detachment of slaves, driven by guards using rifle butts. Suddenly his wife entered his mind. The Cardinal then quoted Frankl's words:

Real or not, her look was then more luminous than the sun which was beginning to rise. A thought transfixed me; for the first time in my life I saw the truth as it is set into song by so many poets, proclaimed as the final wisdom by so many thinkers; that love is the ultimate and the highest goal to which man can aspire. I grasped the meaning of the greatest secret that human poetry and human thought have to impart: the salvation of man is through love and in love.

I understood how a man who has nothing left in the world may still know bliss . . . In utter desolation, when man cannot express himself in positive action, when his only achievement may consist in enduring his suffering in the right way, man can achieve fulfilment. For the first time in my life I was able to understand the meaning of the words, 'The angels are lost in perpetual contemplation of an infinite glory'.

Our child is a Child of the Universe. She can see the invisible. She gives all, to receive all. Like a living flame or a burning torch, she lights the way with her passion for loving. She is God-made-heart. With every beat the vibrations of enfleshed compassion become one with the other and with the ether. And, according to Fyodor Dostoyevski in *The Brothers Karamazov,* nothing or nobody escapes the reach of those infinite arms.

Love people even in their sin, for that is the semblance of Divine Love and is the highest love on earth. Have no fear of human sin. Love all of God's creation, the whole of it and every grain of sand in it. Love every leaf, every ray of God's light. Love the animals, love the plants, love everything. If you love everything, you will perceive the divine mystery in things. Once you perceive it, you will begin to comprehend it better every day. And you will come at last to love the world, always, with an all-embracing love.

Some years ago I was asked to write a *Credo* for a Cosmic Mass in a chapel on a hill overlooking San Francisco Bay. We all got into official trouble over it, both then and later. However, on the occasion of this *Breather,* dedicated to your Child of the Universe, I would like to share it with you now. It is called *Credo in Puellam Aeternam et in Puer Aeternum.* You may wish to use it sometime!

We believe in the child within us.
We believe in her qualities –
>   In openness and wonder
>   In trust and spontaneity
>   In wholeness and immediacy
>   In simplicity and playfulness.
We believe that God is born anew in every birth
and that her heart beats in every child.

We believe that the child within us is wounded.
We believe that until these wounds are healed –
>   We will grow more slowly
>   Love more fearfully
>   Trust more hesitantly
>   Play more seriously
>   And see no miracles.

We believe that God, the Wounded Healer, is forever young
and always loving us into the carefree children we once were.

We believe, because of the Bethlehem Baby, that our Cosmic
Child
is the heart of the Earth and the heart of God; this heart
weeps
>   when innocence is invaded
>   when young trust is betrayed
>   when the land is raped
>   when the elements are abused.

We believe that the child within us and the children around us
– God's small saviours – will one day renew the face of the
earth.

We believe in the Eternal Child, the unlikely prophet in our
hearts,
who teaches us to trust in our passion for the possible,
>   in magic and mystery
>   in fantasy and imagination
>   in letting go and letting be
>   in the impossible dream.

We believe that the music of childhood will once again
empower
dead limbs to move and cosmic feet to dance all night.

We believe, that if we grow truly younger as we grow older,
we will build more surely the Playground of Eternity, where
all creation will run wild with God, for ever and ever. Amen.

Praxis 25

Today, you dance! Or rather move. What else can you do after finishing that *Credo*? Movement can be a fine form of prayer; dance can be pure worship. Clear a little space in your room. Play some lively music, something with a good swing to it, preferably without words. (Ray Lynch's *Deep Breakfast*, for instance, or a Kerry polka!) Wait for a moment to find the feel of it inside you. Try not to think about what to do, which leg to start with or what steps are appropriate. Let the inner rhythm move you; let it lead the way for your body to follow. Swing and sway, jump and dip, gyrate and trot, fast or slow. Do not force the pace but flow at whatever tempo your inside conductor beats out. This exercise is not about proving how acrobatic you are, but about how connected and flowing your mind, body and spirit are. (Do you remember the dance sequence in *Zorba the Greek* or in *Dancing at Lughnasa*?) In other words, be mindful of what is happening. Soon you will notice a wider intimacy with the elements of the universe. Try to feel the music and the dancing and the movement from your still centre. This still place is the centre of gravity located in your stomach, below the navel. According to Eastern wisdom, it is the *t'an tien*, the *hara*, the *ka*, the seat of a powerful energy *(chi)* that is limitless. This is a most therapeutic exercise. There are those who believe that four or five minutes of this activity alone, each morning, is the most beneficial to mind, body and spirit, of all possible uses of meditation time.

Unblock, release and connect

DAY 26 The following three reflections offer a vignette of the actual programme I have followed here at The Spiritual Centre in Little Falls, Minnesota. I offer them to you as *Breathers* during these last days of your month's pilgrimage, to give you a hint of what we experienced here, and as a worthy way of pulling together the themes of our daily reflections thus far.

The sequence, structure and content of the eighteen weeks' course evolved from a single insight – the primacy of the body for holistic living in today's social and religious milieu; the fleshing and incarnating into the muscles, bones, tissues, nerves of my physical self, of the incredibly beautiful revelation that I am lovingly and most delicately fashioned in the image of God. The selection of appropriate explanation and information, varieties of bodywork and hands-on applications, prayer and ritual, recreation and quiet time, emerge from this one central vision. The various segments are all of a piece, fitting together to make a vibrant whole; many patches woven into a seamless garment. This reflection is about how best we can make the journey, live the process at this time in our lives, becoming, in our bodies, what we know in our heads, incarnating more deeply the wisdom of which we are only partially aware. It is about a radical, internal comprehension of, and empathy with, the universal flow of energy that is unconditionally and extravagantly placed at our disposal; all we have to do is to put ourselves in a position to claim it. It is about travelling the path of our bliss towards an ultimate union, intimacy and fusion with the 'Tremendous Lover', whose very breath creates, inflames and satisfies the divine passion for the possible that, deep down, ecstatically consumes our bodies and souls.

The intention is to set free the infinite stream of energy in all of us, so that a state of general well-being will flow through each one and, as a consequence, everyone and everything we touch. To attain to this place of effortless efficiency, much discipline is called for. But for the totally committed and sometimes doubting traveller, the end is sure. While we are learning to swim, for instance, we often think that we will never advance beyond our splashing, floundering, ungainly actions in the water. Then suddenly, one day, when the time is right, we slide into the water and swim away, as confidently as a fish. To be empowered with a new and vibrant energy, after many efforts at mindfulness and body awareness, is something like learning to swim. But, as I have noted throughout the book, you need to be safely held, by loving arms, at the intersection-points of the journey, at the critical moments of the process.

It is important to remember that part of the process of unblocking and integrating the currents of good energy entails the cleansing of the energy channels. As we have already noted, this often forces what is called 'dense, negative energy' to the surface where it gathers and, therefore, has to be released lest it becomes even more intensely toxic. We have touched on this caution already. Writing about the esoteric effects of surrender to God, Peter Roche de Coppens warns that the opening and activation of many higher levels of consciousness through mindfulness, meditation and spiritual exercises, can be an attractive opportunity too, for the forces that wish to destroy all growing and healing. 'It is also the case, that should there be any negative thoughts, emotions and passions (anger, self-pity, jealousy, lust) which have not been purified and transmuted, then, when one experiences the inrush of higher spiritual energies, these negativities can be energised and intensified, wreaking havoc on the life and personality of the seeker.'[35] Older Roman Catholics will remember warnings about lurking devils waiting to catch us off guard! Hence the need for those wise, discerning arms around us.

In this course, and, at certain 'moments' in our lives in general (provided we are awake to those moments) the 'ingredients' for a profound and personal transformation are all strung together in a courageous and powerful way, like the many beads on the one rosary, like the cable-needle picking up the stiches as the new creation is woven into safe wholeness. Our own hearts, those of our friends and all of nature conspire to gift us with health and happiness. Once we are inwardly and outwardly tuned to the vibrations around us, once we are spiritually wired to the network of connections that we cannot see with our eyes alone, then the dormant currents of our energies will be sparked into personal power and inner light. Like the purpose of creation, like the reasons for incarnation, the function of our current explorations is the here and now experience of heaven.

For me, or for anyone embarking on the spiritual adventure, another way of addressing this issue, is to ask whether we really desire to be personally liberated, to be transformed, to be set free from the negative forces in our lives. 'Do you want to be healed?' asked Jesus. Unlike my presence to many other programmes and workshops, this time, for a variety of reasons, I have committed myself totally to its aims and goals, its vision and tactics. In recent years I have heard so many leaders, prophets and pioneers say to the gathered followers who had shown interest in some project or enterprise, 'It will work if you want it to work. Do you *really* and *truly* want this movement, dream, adventure to become a reality? Because if you do, it will happen.'

Without extreme effort, work-pressure, straining, or forcing of the river, I try, like an alert rabbit or squirrel sitting still, to hold myself in relaxed readiness, yet eternally vigilant and effortlessly poised, with full attention and awareness so as not to miss a connecting moment, a magic bridge, a passing angel's message, a drum-beat of revelation – the uniting breath that begins and continues the transfiguration of my life. There is no stress, anxiety or pressure in this attention to what gathers and connects us to God. This uniting breath is like an inner homing device, that draws us backwards and forwards, to the Divine Essence, from whence we came in the beginning. This, I suppose, is the original meaning of the word 'religion' – from the Latin *religare*, to re-fasten, or to re-connect with our essential nature.

I'm sure it will help when I give some practical examples of what I mean by a dedicated presence, a total commitment to the quest for inner freedom. Today we embarked on a special project – the making of a drum. From past experience I'm well aware that this could have been, for me, just a somewhat interesting part of the course, a job to be done, something I was expected to participate in. Or, by my personal preparation for this adventure, through meditation, reading and sincere openness to the Spirit of the Mystery, it could be a vital and holy propulsion to speed me on my journey in pursuit of my bliss. I can whole-heartedly enter into the spiritual exercise of making the drum, praying the process, believing that I'm purifying and re-creating my inner being in a loving, respectful and joyful meditation.

It is at this breakthrough moment, I believe, that the empowering connecting with all the other precious, significant 'moments' of this course, explodes into vivifying and positive energy. As I touched and shaped the moist deer-skin for the creation of my drum today, and wondered about the cry of the lovely animal as it was accidentally killed, I remembered that every morning since I came here, I have recited, sometimes aloud, a Celtic prayer that has nourished and sustained me, called *The Deer's Cry*. The cry of the deer resonated in the early centuries in Ireland, it sounded during the Tenebrae of the first Good Friday when all creation cried out, and was heard, for the very first time, on the fifth day of creation.

In the beginning was the Drum
And the Drum was with God
And the Drum was God.

There is no easy way to hear the song of the universe, no short-cuts to the light on the mountain, no primer to teach us how to read the mystery in a stone, no magic blessing or curse to banish the demons from our hearts. Any form of enlightenment can only be achieved by a form of dying. How easily we say and shape such words but, because we shy away from the experience, we miss their meaning. To reach a state of emptiness, of poverty of heart, is such a hard-won position that is never secure. To surrender our ego-castle, to unblock the personal pride, to make space for the universal energy to flood our souls, is the adventure of the saint. And there can be no fullness without the emptiness, no giving out before a giving in, no breakthrough before a breakdown, no invisible protection of the angels before the painstaking dismantling of the self-protective armour of the ego.

Before we can be played upon by the Spirit, into the clear, sweet music of the abundant life, there must be, as with the hollowed reed, a lot of scraping and shaping, cleansing and crafting, so that every part of us can resonate, in tune and in rhythm, in time and in tempo, with the true vibrations of God's breath. It is because of this trial by fire, this desert experience, this living out of our personal Good Friday, that the journey home to ourselves and to God is not to be taken lightly. Without the tangible, reassuring comfort of the true love of our family or of a genuinely devoted community, or of an *anam chara* or loved one, there is the very real danger of getting lost in the dark.

Oh my heart, because I love you
You will never die.
My darling, when the storms blow
Remember what I said.

Praxis 26

The Gaelic word *anamchara* means a 'soul-friend', a true mentor
– one who loves you without being jealous, who guides you
without being judgmental, who walks beside you without trying to change your pace. Today's meditation is about discerning
the one who plays that role in your life. Your *anamchara* is the
person who makes the above reflection come true, the one who
convinces you of your own heart-power. I suggest that in your
prayer today you decide to deeply appreciate in your life that
one person who stands by you, who believes in you, who affirms and encourages you, and who does not look for a reward
from you. You are lucky beyond measure, and the world envies
you, if you can identify such a person. Part of your anxiety may
spring from the fact that you cannot name an *anamchara*. Maybe
there is someone who wishes to take that role but does not feel
invited by you. Maybe it is only when you, yourself, nurture the
energy to walk with someone else, becoming their guiding angel
in a totally altruistic and sensitive way, that you too will receive
this precious gift. In your prayer today reflect on Jesus' need of
close and intimate friends, those women and men whose touch
he needed – there was one who washed his feet and dried them
with her hair, and the other who laid his head on his chest. These
may have been the intimate touches that helped Jesus continue
his mission when his spirits were low.

Don't miss the moment

DAY 27

While these last *Breathers* arise from reflections on my recent spiritual journey in the USA, they equally apply to all our current travels along the path of our bliss. I asked myself many questions. Am I totally committed to the surrender of my life to God? Am I dedicated to becoming aware of the immense possibility for personal transformation in every moment and in every place? I think of how a mother, all through every night, and maybe through her own illness, is unceasingly aware of the needs of her sick child; I think even of the sacrificial schedule and punishing routine, year after year, of someone in training for Olympic gold. I am in a privileged space these weeks to come to myself. I too have a child in need within me; I too have a golden light to strive for and claim. Without becoming a burden to myself or a nuisance to others, no matter how busy life seems, am I availing myself of the fertile and fleeting opportunities of grace each moment of each day, both now and tomorrow?

I'm referring here to the everyday experiences of such common activities as looking, breathing, moving. Take, for example, the suggestions we received here on our arrival, about the sacredness of eating. After years of standing-up cups of tea for breakfast and take-away pizzas just before midnight, to savour the flavour of food, in a civilised and reflective way, was a new experience. To reflect a little about where and by whom the wheat was harvested, the tea processed, the animals killed and their meat prepared. To notice the taste of things, the hot and cold of things, the soft and the chewy bits, was a new kind of slowing down for me, a new awareness, a new blessing. And then to connect that awareness with the rest of our experiences – feelings, thoughts, actions, reactions. We need to realise the frantic speed of our lives and change it in order to be; we need a different life-rhythm if we are to notice and feel each physical and mental movement, each expression of emotion, each silence. We need to *practise* awareness so that it becomes a kind of second nature to us. Some kind of habitual change in the way we perceive our environment must happen if we are ever to be attentive to the ordinary and the unusual, to the hundreds of small miracles we take for granted, to the sacrament of the present moment.

In our *T'ai Chi Chih* practices, for instance, the aim is to un-block, to release the flow and to connect the energies within. The practised movements open a way for the trapped and hidden self to be recreated. They require attention and concentration at every second until they become second nature. They bring a new awareness of the length and stretch of our limbs and mus-cles. The practice of this art creates connections between outer energy and inner wisdom. As I gave my full mind to practising with my friends, I tried to *feel* the connections with my inner wisdom, to *experience* my emerging self, to hear the voice of my inner child. Maybe this is one of the places of truth, of what Joseph Campbell called the 'homeland of the muses, the inspirer of the arts.' If you ask around, you will be surprised at the num-ber of people who, out of the sheer need for staying sane and together, have a regular pattern of some such prayerful series of actions or meditations each day.

Yesterday in the pool, instead of forcing some more lengths from my tired body, I deliberately felt the texture and support of the water, moving my hands through its gentle resistance, and connected it with this morning's ritual about the mystery and power of water in our lives. I tried not to take the water for granted, as simply something to swim in, but as the wonderful womb of life, as the symbol of rebirth, of fresh and green begin-nings. I saw my adventure with the water (likewise after a shower, a bath, a face-wash, a car-wash) as part of the regeneration going on within me and thanked it for the huge part it was playing in my life. By incorporating and connecting the wisdom of the water, of my body, mind and spirit with all my other exper-iences these days, I simply knew that an immense power was being set free to bring me to a place I had never been before. I remember, too, the lavish sprinkling of holy water by my mother, last thing at night, on the occasion of leaving home, before be-ginning something new, during a storm – whether of winds or words.

Just as we did during our course here, it is important, wher-ever we find ourselves, to create fine channels of connection between the life-giving sources of each day. Or when holding the bread and wine at the eucharist, instead of my usual habits of thought, I slow down and deliberately make myself aware of

the archetypal nature of these universal symbols, risking opening myself to what seers like Joseph Campbell would describe as
the mythical power of fire, light and soul-consuming, creative
energies available to our deepest selves in this ritual. It is not so
much the meaning of life that is important, they say, it is the experience of being alive. The function of life is to lead us to its
own rapture. We are called to create our own reality. Because we
have God's presence in our bodies, God's energy in our minds
and hearts, the only limits set are those we draw out of our own
fear. How often do we really *feel* our soul, with its passion for the
possible? How often do we find, with the poet, an invincible
summer at the heart of our winter? How often are we suddenly
surprised by the courage of our capacity, not just to suffer
tragedies, but to grow and blossom through them?

Last night, unbidden, another powerful ally placed its rich
resources at my disposal in the form of a dream. Even during the
night the connecting can keep happening. Our dreams are amazing connectors and their wisdom is honoured and respected
when we explore some of the revealing and healing significance
of the symbols and archetypes which fill them. Briefly, it was
about my delight to be with a group of young, hippie-type,
happy people, and particularly my rapport with a golden-
haired poet who accompanied me on a journey to a local church,
with a bottle of wine that I was asked to supply for Mass. Along
the way I saw a grey funeral heading towards the church with a
traditional monsignor officiating. Our journey was through a
difficult tunnel and as we approached the church I realised that I
had lost the wine. Full of panic, we retraced our steps searching
frantically for the lost bottle, at which point I woke up. One way
of exploring the dream was to see all the characters in it as aspects of myself and, in mythical terms, to see the bottle of wine
as the real truth. Was the truth to be found and consumed with
the creative and colourful people or in a dark-grey church?
What a creative, intriguing way of imaging the internal struggle
for integrity within myself! The dream was clearly another
emergence of the subconscious self stirred into consciousness by
all the happenings of these days.

If one word only could be used to sum up the aim of all the
elements of our course, it would be *awareness*. Having read all
the books and hand-outs, seen all the videos, worked through
the Parental and Enneagram weeks, breathed our way into the

Holotropic day, persisted with the *T'ai Chi Chih* movements, the voice, sound, mask-making and drum practices, experienced the *Reiki* and *Feldenkrais* empowerments, explored our *chakra* centres – the one personal transformation that connects all these experiences could be named as the condition of awareness. While the focus of the process is none other than a shift in the way we are present to our lives, this presence and this awareness marks the beginning of the inner work, not the end. In my meditation I pray, as we are exhorted to do in the Hebrew scriptures, that this transformed consciousness will adhere to my bones, become flesh of my flesh, be incorporated radically into the very texture of my heart and body.

True awareness is a rare gift, yet it is accessible to all. It is regarded as the grace that transcends the ego, the blessing that transforms our level of self-acceptance and, consequently, our self-esteem. It is the litmus paper that reveals the life-long pattern of our insecurity, our anxiety and fear, our anger and resentment, our envy and jealousy, our critical and blaming habits. It is an extraordinary kind of skill, or aptitude, or facility, to begin noticing our spontaneous reactions, to catch our split-second, off-guard emotions in the face of some sudden happening, to be attentive to our body movements and tensions at any given time for whatever reason, to watch the unfailing way we respond, at a compulsory, driven level to certain kinds of people, stimuli, behaviour, information. Life is happening to us all the time; our awareness is often absent. And, as we have considered already, once we are aware of what is going on within us, the healing and wholeness naturally and supernaturally follows, without any extreme efforts or desperate strategies on our part. Breather 31 and Praxis 31 will develop this truth more fully.

Praxis 27

Only that day dawns to which we are fully awake. Today, try to get
your various energies flowing together in the following way.
(We began a simpler version of this practice two weeks ago.)
Vigorously rub your hands together and place them on different
parts of your body. Stimulate your face and scalp, tweaking,
pinching and kneading your eyebrows, your ears, your cheek-
bones, your chin-line, the side of your nose. All of these spruce
up your skin and affect all kinds of organs and their functions
throughout your body. Do all of this gently and lovingly. And
talk to the places you are touching. Thank them for their loyal
service to you. It is not silly to do this. We often stay stuck in
mediocrity because we fear the comments of cynical acquaint-
ances. What a dreadful way to stay a victim! Your body is your
best friend throughout your life; it is also your portable and
faithful home. Now rub your hands together again, to generate
more energy or *chi*, and slap yourself briskly all over – back, but-
tocks, front, up and down your legs. Notice your breathing.
Place your feet together and move your hips and pelvis in a circle.
For various reasons these are often the neglected areas of our
bodies, yet they contain so many of our vital organs. Imagine
you are keeping a hula-hoop spinning at waist-level. Breathe as
normally as you can. Sit down now and feel the energy radiating
within and around you. Slowly make the Sign of the Cross, or
some other 'closing gesture', to bring it all together and to complete your salutation to your body, to God and to the new day.

Be an alchemist

DAY 28

There are a thousand opportunities every day for each one of us to encounter the negative reactions in our lives, to transform the ego, to cut another link in the chains that bind us, to feel the fear and do it anyway, to listen to our bodies and our inner voices. During all our waking hours, our senses are unceasingly carrying messages to our brain and we are responding, reacting and 'proacting' constantly. Every single, slightest moment brings us an opportunity to either deepen the rut in which we find ourselves or to take another 'giant stride of soul' along the path of our bliss. Like a serious game it is both exciting and demanding. You know beyond doubt that you are at the interface of fear and freedom, powerlessness and power, resentment and acceptance, victimhood and self-acceptance. Beyond the state of knowing something cerebrally, this interface has a unique, experiential bite to it. Many can read or write about an apple; only you can actually taste your apple.

As I daily become more alert to these precious moments, their number increases. The exercise of noticing what you are doing, feeling, saying, thinking is not an intrusive distraction that mitigates the intensity or sincerity of whatever is going on. Because at such all-too-rare occasions I am moving in a raised kind of consciousness; I become more aware of *everything* that is going on, and my relaxation, in the middle of it all, only increases. As I try to spend more time in this transformed sense of presence to everyone, and everything, and to life itself, I feel again, that it has to do with an almost cosmic kind of connecting. This springs from a number of graced attitudes. One of these is what St Thomas called 'magnanimity'. This, I believe, is the virtue of extravagance and abundance, of surrender and of 'giving ourselves over', of radiating our beautiful light outwards with no thought of what happens to it, or whether or not it is ever received.

There must be a compassionate whole-heartedness in the way we throw ourselves into the art of awareness. We are called to give this 'enterprise of the soul', this pearl of great price, our most vital energy, the fullness of our being, our most precious presence. Because what is sought for is that 'condition of simplicity costing not less than everything', there is a very obvious reluctance to 'sell everything' else, a profound resistance to becoming a temporary but necessary victim of sacrifice. There is an understandable holding back, a fearful clinging to safety, a foggy uncertainty that makes the full, exciting dawn of awareness almost impossible to witness. I am personally convinced of the truth of the perception that it is only when we take the leap of faith with abandonment that the wind blows fair to fill our sails. It is only when we plunge into the abyss of our ego's terror and throw away our only compass as we push off from the familiar but insufficient shore, that our guardian angels swoop ever so low above our heads, to guide and draw us into the previously unknown and even unsuspected territories and horizons of our soul. It is an aching, breaking, ecstatic, valley-low, mountain-high adventure.

Without a wild trusting in the ultimate One who connects all, who *is* connection, the unblocking and emptying, the releasing, the reaching out and the coming together cannot happen. To trust in the present moment and in the potential growing and healing in my awareness of it, I must first find a place to trust within myself. This, in turn, has something to do with how loved and loveable I think I am. So many weeds of doubt, self-hatred, dislikes, subtle competing, criticising and manoeuvring are alive, like toxic viruses, poisoning the small buds of promise in the garden of our souls. Unknowingly, we stay stuck in these awful traps and prisons of judging and jealousy, and unless and until they are sprung (and they can only be sprung and unlocked from within, and nobody is ultimately without the graced capacity to achieve this) the deadly cycle will never be broken in our own particular lifetime. Too many strings are being held on to, too many calculations being made, too many tapes of caution are playing around in my head. Letting go of the deeply entrenched desire to control needs a miracle of grace. Because I'm afraid, I must manipulate. Every voice from my childhood years, belonging to parent, teacher and priest, rises to screaming pitch the nearer I get to the moment of irreversible decision, the point of one-way departure, the last disentangling of the hands that cling to me and will not let go. May I remind you again of *The Journey* by Mary Oliver:

One day you finally knew
what you had to do, and began,
though the voices around you
kept shouting
their bad advice –
though the whole house
began to tremble
and you felt the old tug
at your ankles.
"Mend my life!"
each voice cried.
But you didn't stop.[36]

It seems to me that my consciousness is transformed by my attention to the present moment, by my awareness of what is happening just now, by noticing all that is going on in my head and heart and body each instant of my day. There is no other time to *feel* my soul, to encounter my dragon, to become my grace. That is what we mean by *kairos* time as opposed to *chronos* time. There is a sacred timelessness *(kairos)* to each chronological second *(chronos)* if we are but alive to the here and now unfolding of mystery's moments. Grace builds on nature and it is only through our daily, human experiences in time and space, that the sacred can be revealed.

Through every cleft, the world we perceive floods us with its richness – food for the body, nourishment for the eyes, the harmony of sounds and fullness of heart, unknown phenomena and new truths – all these treasures, all these stimuli, all these calls coming to us from the four corners of the world, cross our consciousness at every moment. What is their role within us? They will merge into the most intimate life of our soul, and either develop it or poison it.[37]

Praxis 28

Find one of your favourite candles and light it. Do this deliberately and in a meditative way. I suggest that you perform this small but profound action at each morning practice. When performed with deep awareness, it is a complete prayer and an act of worship in itself. As you gaze at the quiet power of the little candle, ask yourself about your own inner light. What is it that shines inside you even at awkward or ambiguous times throughout the day? What are the principles that have been a constant in your life, when faced with immediate and difficult decisions? Is it a sense of fairness, of justice, of standing up for the underdog? Do you notice a feeling of compassion for the 'sinner', a kind of realisation that you too could be in that place? Is there a deep-seated attitude of thanksgiving for your life and the life of the world, a sense of wonder that you are there at all? Make a list of no more than two or three of your abiding princi ples, your guiding lights which, even under temptation and pressures, never go out for very long. Read them aloud to yourself. These give the brightest witness to the presence of the Holy Spirit in your soul. Let them resonate in your body all day. Those who practice *Reiki* absorb the following ideals into their inner being: Just for today, I will not be angry. Just for today, I will not worry. Just for today, I will give thanks for my many blessings.

Embrace your shadow

DAY 29 It is not yet one o'clock in the afternoon. Let me briefly review some of the golden opportunities that already have gifted one of my ordinary days here, where the young Mississippi river tests its strength, with wide, looping swings across the plains, and then, just beyond Little Falls, after a swirling moment of playful rest, it begins its long, long journey southwards through the vast country of the United States before surrendering itself blissfully into the warm body of the Gulf of Mexico. So, I woke up early today, delighted at the prospect of a free morning. Suddenly I remembered that I had a nine o'clock appointment. Immediately I felt frustration, self-pity and resentment at both myself, for agreeing to, and at the other person, for asking for, the meeting. Equally quickly I became aware of what was going on inside me – the energy wasted in blaming, in resisting the reality of the situation, in missing the moment. And simply because of that conscious awareness, in a moment, truly, it was over. The instant we detach ourselves from the emotion, we are free of its power. The time and money you have spent on this book will have been well rewarded, if you remember that fact alone. We are no longer victimised by any negative feeling once we become aware that we are feeling it. This awareness brings us back to our centre, grounded and secure.

I then went to the kitchen. Just as the kettle was boiling, and the microwave with my porridge in it went 'ping', the telephone rang. Immediately I became a martyr, impatient and irritated at the lack of consideration on the caller's part. Even before I reached the phone, I had noticed what was going on. I was allowing someone else to decide my moods, giving someone control over this precious moment, and this person may even be calling to tell me something wonderful. In an instant I felt centred and took the call with genuine grace. I returned to the kitchen and the opening words of the first person I encountered after I finished my Quaker Oats were, 'Haven't seen much of you lately, stranger. Where have you been?' Ouch! I blazed inwardly. Bitch! A perfect bull's eye. Right on the button. My body went tense. I was being judged. I did not belong. This was pressure all right – the pressure of guilt and anger.

It was at this point that I became aware of my turmoil; I felt my tension; sensed my rage. In this awareness I put a distance between myself and my feelings. That was the key to 'coming back to myself'. All of this went through my mind in the time it takes to draw a few breaths. Then those negative shadows melted away. They just evaporated. Sounds like magic. The process of distancing them and naming them, drained them of their power. It is well known that the essential lifespan of such eruptions of emotion is only a few seconds in duration. After that, by splicing on to the coils of other unprocessed and buried feelings, they take on a different and destructive life of their own, and can become an almost unending rope of wrath. Looking back now, I remember thinking about how much inner work I still had to do in that area, how unprotected I was, how unfree. And, as a result of this, I feel a sense of gratitude for the unsuspecting person who brought about this new awareness.

It is still only eight forty-five! Before my appointment, and feeling very pleased with myself, I made a quick visit to the Great Hall where a few of my friends were putting the finishing touches to the painting of our new drums. As I admired one really pretty one in particular, and glanced over to my own seemingly unattractive one, I suddenly knew that I was becoming anxious, even distressed. In my automatic comparisions between the two, I was definitely losing. Even before my first conscious thought about what was happening inside me, a whole life's history of apprehension about not being good enough, about failure, about having to compete and win, had played itself out in my body and my emotions. Within seconds I had the tightening, sickly reactions identified and purified. I was able to honestly and freely praise the lovely work of art.

After my appointment I'm walking along the middle corridor. It is eleven o'clock. Time for a cup of coffee before coming up here to continue with these reflections. We're well into our programme by now and I'm thinking how well I'm doing. Good course! Well worth the money! Delightful people! My body feels so good today! It obviously loves the way I'm listening to it! Someone is coming down the stairs. 'Good morning . . .' I sing out, feeling very loved by everyone here. No reply. Scarcely a glance. She walks on. I'm dumbstruck. If this happened to you,

you would probably have shrugged your shoulders at this rather common occurrence and probably made some excuse for the cold behaviour. But I'm transfixed. I feel the chill of fear in my chest. I'm rejected, cut off. I'm hated. I look around furtively, hoping nobody else saw the incident. I have always needed to be liked, accepted, appreciated. But this is not happening now. Maybe I don't belong here. Maybe I should quit the course early!

All these negative charges carried the force of electric shocks to my guts. They happened in the space of a few steps, a few long seconds. Then I spoke to myself quietly about taking responsibility for my own part of the encounter (or non-encounter!). I had acted in good faith. I really liked the person in question. There were probably many reasons for her to be preoccupied or even depressed. And then my stabbing feelings were there no longer. They were over. I paused again and realised that the causes for my reaction were as old as humanity. The seeds of my needy feelings – to be accepted by everybody, to be liked, to be loved, to be popular – were planted into my system as, cradled in my mother's loving arms, I greedily sucked in her milk.

In this context, I need to mention one more, recent, discovery, that has brought much delight, even though 'living the discovery' will take, at least, a lifetime. As I become more clearly aware, especially since I came here to the Centre, of my mental and emotional responses and reactions across a wide range of encounters, discussions and challenges, I notice surprisingly strong tendencies arising within me – a haste to defend myself unnecessarily, to react in a touchy and prickly manner, to be too easily 'hurt' by mistakenly taking things personally, to be silently resentful, to blame and criticise more often than I would like to admit. These are nearly all negative and damaging. They are blockages to the flow of divine light and energy through my body and soul.

While I always suspected that I carry more than my fair share of the fall-out of original sin, I never suspected, through familiarity with it, that so much of the furniture in my living-room was so riddled with wood-worm! Like the doctor who finds the point of death-dealing blockage in one of the patient's veins or arteries, or like the engineer who traces the obstruction in the life-giving water-supply to a wasting community, I too was delighted to become aware of these obstacles to grace, deep within my being, but dismayed at their stubborn power and 'squatters' rights' persistence. The cause of my joy is this: if the destination of my hero's journey is beginning to clarify itself, if my reasons for the spiritual quest are simplifying themselves at last, then I am encouraged to trust, let go and live in the present moment even further. Put another way, if it is being revealed to me that the essence of my life is love, that I'm called and drawn to a challenging and demanding commitment to serve and to be in the holy presence of the *anawim* (the poor, the marginalised, the lonely, the homeless,) then, through God's unconditional graciousness, I find a peace in the way my life is unfolding, and a new heart for exploring what lies beyond the immediate horizon.

Praxis 29

Settle yourself down – it is another new day. When you are ready, reflect on the way you tend to handle one or other of the situations such as I recalled above. If none of them would extend your patience, common sense or wisdom, think of an event that would. Have you noticed any positive change in how you respond, for instance, to the sudden challenge? To notice and distance oneself from the rushing, sometimes overwhelming emotions that seem to come from nowhere, takes patience and determination. It takes much trial and error to be attentive to what all our lives we have not explored, examined or noticed. This precious approach or habit will be further developed in *Breather Thirty One*. Just for today, try again to cultivate a mindfulness about your moment-to-moment feelings. What is important is to dismantle their power over you, to see them as separate from your own essence. First you become aware of your agitation, anxiety, frustration, impatience, exasperation. Then you use the breathing space to establish the more appropriate response of your own choice. The mature response, I am suggesting, will begin with holding the emotion without judgement or expectation. Today's praxis is about reminding ourselves to develop a stillness within us – at all times, if possible – so as to notice, without straining, all that is going on in our minds, hearts and bodies.

Live in the present

DAY 30

Our true home is in the present moment.
To live in the present moment is a miracle.
The miracle is not to walk on water.
The miracle is to walk on the green Earth in the present moment.

These words by Thich Nhat Hanh about returning to the present moment from wherever you have strayed, is our theme for *Breather* Thirty. You will notice how the theme is spread throughout the book. It is also spread throughout the theologies, mysticism and wisdom of the great world religions. As well as everything else, it makes good sense. It is extraordinary how much time we spend worrying over future possibilities or regretting things from our past lives. We waste huge amounts of precious energy over useless anxiety. No wonder we feel drained and tired so often. This *Breather* is another reminder about coming to your senses, literally – to what you are currently seeing, hearing and touching. This is the safest and surest place to be. No one can harm you if you abide in the here and now. It is also the only meeting-place between you and the God called *I am*; the only moment of encounter between our spirits and the Spirit of all life. It is uniquely in the here and now that the pen-point of God's love writes on the page of our humanity, as the divine drama of the incarnation unfolds.

It is only from the vantage-point of the naked 'now' that we can discern the countryside through which we are travelling. It is, in fact, the time for literally taking a 'breather' with deep breaths, for letting the shoulders sag, for stopping the desperate pushing and relentless demanding with which we drive our fragile bodies and minds.

'Stay here,' advises Rumi, the medieval Persian prophet, 'quivering with each moment, like a drop of mercury.' And quite miraculously, once we actually stop the urgent and intense doing, it is as though we are healed automatically by graced life itself; without actually 'doing' anything, we swiftly regain a refreshing balance that provides a new energy to continue the journey. Many times a day, especially when I'm drawn to anxiety or doubt, I fall back on this gospel counsel. Because this blessed ability to stay in the present is reached through the grace of trusting and letting go, it has an immediate effect on body and soul. Whenever I'm asked to sum up, in a sentence, what 'works for me', I tend to repeat that last sentence.

At dozens of workshops that I have either organised or participated in, tired people seem to be worn out from trying to be good, striving to be better, proving their worth and therefore, competing with either themselves or others. It is a deadly trap. Our religious upbringing has often contributed to this malaise. We were told that we must earn and merit God's love. Too much talk about God's unconditional love for us, it was felt, would make us all careless and irresponsible, sending us wildly out of control, abusing and taking for granted this tender, divine love. Jesus would not agree. Mary Oliver does not see it that way either:

You do not have to be good.
You do not have to walk on your knees
for a hundred miles through the desert, repenting.
You only have to let the soft animal of your body
       love what it loves.
Tell me about despair, yours, and I will tell you mine.
Meanwhile the world goes on.
Meanwhile the sun and the clear pebbles of the rain
are moving across the landscapes,
over the prairies and the deep trees,
the mountains and the rivers.
Meanwhile the wild geese, high in the clear blue air
are heading home again.
Whoever you are, no matter how lonely,
the world offers itself to your imagination,
calls to you like the wild geese, harsh and exciting –
over and over announcing your place
in the family of things.[38]

Three hundred years ago, Jean Pierre de Caussade SJ reminded his students that no moment is trivial since every moment contains 'a divine kingdom and heavenly sustenance' within it. He believed with a passion that the only reliable breather was 'the sacrament of the present moment'. When we succeed in 'living in the now', however, it is far more than simply escaping into a momentary oasis of peace. There are almost unbelievable implications that we can scarcely imagine. Archbishop Thomas Menamparampil believes this:

What gives you a grip into the immense universe and the entire course of history is your present moment and your present task. Your faithful use of the present moment and your fidelity to today's task makes you plug your 'now' into God's 'eternal now'. And with that you achieve the impossible. You can be truly with everyone in every place. You can be involved in everything as you reach out in all directions. Time and space disappear. You can carry God's love to anyone in any part of the world.[39]

Such unconditional surrender to God's will as revealed in each passing second requires immense trust. Yesterday, when the sun shone and my spirits were high, I found myself trying to lock into that moment and preserve it forever. That is not the way to live in the present, where we take it on trust that the future can be safely left in God's tender hands. We know well that we are incapable of faith like that, but once we risk pushing out the boat, the wind of the Spirit blows with unexpected intensity. For now, if you are not already familiar with this belief and practice, I encourage you to reflect on it. The present moment is the only truth. It is where everything good happens. It is free of the memories and fears that keep blotting the sun from our lives. Our guardian angels guard it safely. But we must find it. It takes vigilance and costs not less than everything.

Where shall I look for enlightenment?
Here.
When will it happen?
It is happening right now.
Then why don't I experience it?
Because you do not look.
What should I look for?
Nothing. Just look.
At what?
Anything your eyes alight upon.
Must I look in a special kind of way?
No. The ordinary way will do.
But don't I always look the ordinary way?
No.
Whyever not?
Because to look you must be here.
You are mostly somewhere else.[40]

Praxis 30

The temptation to give up on the fixed time for meditation each day will be great. This inner discipline can be difficult and demanding. Our minds are like jumping monkeys and hyperactive grasshoppers. So sit or lie down again and, this time, notice, as you do so, the sensations and pressure-points in your body, in your feet touching the floor, or back touching the chair, the tension in your face, the warmth where your limbs are folded over – elbows, back of knees, armpits. Can you bring your attention to any part of your body that you decide? Bring your mantra or favourite phrase before your inner eye, or focus on your breathing, counting your breaths if you find it helpful. Gently acknowledge all the thoughts, images and feelings that cross your mind and heart, and quietly let them slip away. Simply continue to do this. Maintain your awareness of what is going on in your mind, heart, body and breathing. Do not get stuck in any inside debate. Keep letting go. Begin with your toes and travel up through your body. There is no need for any results or conclusions. This is a 'coming home' to your body, your mind, your truest self. Let there be a flow about this kind of mindfulness. It has a power for conditioning us positively and profoundly. This conscious awareness will have a tremendous effect in the quality of your presence to everyone, and to everything, throughout the day ahead. You will, of course, if you're anything like me, keep forgetting. Patiently, begin again.

Travelling light

DAY 31

When we are travelling light, the divine light we carry within us is set free to travel as well. The title of the book is about the letting go of the baggage of our lives and also about the travelling light that we bring to the dark places. Today's final *Breather* is an attempt to explain how I understand one of the main processes for making headway along our often dim paths of pain into God's light. These paths of pain may be crowded with the regular traffic of minor annoyances, frustrations and irritations with which we are all familiar, or they may be peopled with raw, searing memories that stretch back a long way. 'Offer it up!' was a popular piece of devotional advice for tormented souls in past decades. 'Look at the Cross!' was another. Contemporary sophisticated Roman Catholics tend to dismiss such pious practices as rather old-fashioned, simplistic and ineffectual. *Breather* Thirty One, however, explores one way of understanding a hidden richness in such phrases and exhortations. In doing this, it also pulls together many strands and themes scattered throughout the days of the month in the pages of this book.

We have already touched, in the preceding *Breathers*, on various ways of encountering and discerning the levels of darkness and light along the inner journey of our lives. These ways and skills have, in general, a number of common characteristics. Among such 'givens' I emphasise the following:

i) noticing / awareness,
ii) separating / distancing,
iii) holding / waiting,
iv) understanding / enlightenment,
v) loving / compassion.

After many decades of trial and error, what follows now is one person's tentative attempt to weave together into a seamless robe, these redeeming and liberating graces of healing and growing.

As I watch myself, the first thing that happens as a result of a disturbing and hurtful experience is the perceived impact (charge) of my defensive resistance – that is, denial, fear, shame, anger, hurt, impatience, loss or frustration. For a moment it is all one flash of experience, as mental, physical and emotional reactions come together. What happens next is my conscious awareness of what is happening in me. Sometimes, in the past, this awareness, this noticing took ages. I would brood, wallow, be anxious and out of kilter for days. How long does it take to quieten down the wild, bucking horse beneath me? How long to disentangle my foot from the hawser that is dragging me into the sea? Issues around shame, for instance, have notoriously deep and twisted tentacles. Now, by practising attentiveness/awareness, I break through the blind force of negative emotion more quickly. On a good day, I notice my agitation, jealousy or resentment straight away.

To notice so as to separate
In the traditional spiritual manuals of my seminary days, this current practice of 'living in the now', of attending and noticing, used to be called 'the sacrament of the present moment' or the grace of self-awareness. The 'enlightened', those we called saints, through the virtue of 'detachment' (another 'classic' virtue – currently referred to as 'letting go') could do it very swiftly. Jesus could do it almost immediately. 'Father if it be possible, let this chalice pass from me *but* . . .' For most of us, however, it takes longer. Until our souls are more open and more sensitive to God's purifying touch, we have to travel carefully, step by step. What follows is an attempt to track and trace in our consciousness, those movements of grace in our soul.

The moment the negative emotion is recognised and accepted, the true self returns to the centre. (Somewhat like the inattentive goalkeeper, realising he has been enticed out the field in the heat of the moment, quickly scurries back to where he is rightfully centred, between his grounded goal-posts.) Now I can choose. Now I can be compassionate to myself and others. The *awareness* of the fact that '*I* am angry' meaning 'I *have* anger', '*I* am afraid' meaning 'I *have* fear', rather than 'I *am* the anger', 'I *am* the fear', breaks the awesome power of the sudden rage, the 'red mist'. What is to be avoided is our becoming identified with the emotion, our being taken over by the strength of our reaction. This is a condition of being possessed by our demons and unbaptised energies. When this happens we are at the mercy of our passions, out of control, in fact, slaves to whatever rages in our soul. When, however, I can say '*I* am angry' meaning '*I* am in charge of this emotion', '*I* am in the driving seat', only then can we regain our mature humanity, respond appropriately and avoid doing or saying something that we may regret for many a day. To arrive at this authentic place of balance means that I am now no longer driven by the anger or fear; that I am quickly responsible (response-able), that I am out of the ego, my false self and into the essence, my true self. (The unfocused goalkeeper is no longer hopelessly stranded and astray at midfield; he is back between his posts where he is centred and flexible.)

Without the alchemy of awareness, this is the blind moment when awful and irrevocable things are said and done. What is not identified and owned will be dangerously and wildly projected. As in the mixed happenings of most of my days, this separation, this detachment of myself from my feelings, is sufficient to restore me to my inner peace and equilibrium. Through observing, noticing, I no longer identify with my negative emotion. I am more than it. This searing sensation, this powerful feeling is but a part of me. It is not my whole self. My true self is untouched. When I realise this, I give myself space to turn, room to choose. This is a crucial moment in the process. Once I have choice, I am free. The most important factor is not the nature of the actual change (if any) in my external behaviour or the eventual, practical outcome in terms of the relationship or experience in question, but the liberating, individuating process of finally identifying what is authentic and true, what is 'really real', and then of making a free, personal choice. I offer one example of how I recently explored this sequence of transforming graces:

During a day's conference with priests on the theme of 'The Priest as Puppet' (contrasting our graced responses to the gentle strings of God's whispers with our fearful, knee-jerk reactions to the judgmental strings of others), I worked through the following scenario with them. Even though we may not admit to it, as a rule, we priests are very sensitive to people's comments about our homilies. A complimentary remark can 'make our day' and a 'thumbs-down' response is usually taken very personally. Suppose, I said, that at the end of the retreat, the majority of those priests present informed me in no uncertain terms that they regarded the day as a wash-out, a complete waste of time. How would I feel? How would I work with the feeling? How would I transform those emotions?

First of all I am shocked, hurt, angry, fearful – probably in that order. Then, as I drive home, I distance myself from those negative emotions, without necessarily naming them too soon, draw a deep breath, 'sit in the clearing' and try to trust and wait in that non-blaming space. Every so often the sense of embarrassment and resentment returns. Without getting worked up about them, or judging them, I let them quietly recede again. Gradually it begins to dawn on me that I do not depend on my successes and the passing approvals of those I encounter, for my happiness or self-esteem. This awareness is like springing the trap of my victimhood. It is like a real taste of true resurrection. My real self-esteem is now based on something else, or rather on someone else – not so much on what those around me think of me as I stand before them, but on how I stand before God and before myself.

During the rest of the evening, at home, (I explained to the assembled priests) what I noticed coming out of the clearing was not, anymore, the wild creatures of my shame, anxiety and anger but the revealing creatures of the trapped dimensions of my life – my insecurity, my need of praise, my low self-esteem. The names of my emotions – what crept into the clearing – had changed already. They were now the names of the cells I lived in. And all the cells were hacked out of the heavy walls of the prison of fear. A whole new context was emerging. Profound insights were beginning to clarify themselves. Then, as the evening wore on, (and as I stayed in the clearing) the features and names of the animals changed yet again. Now they were more like guide-dogs, homing doves, guardian angels, glowing lanterns, moving ahead and inviting me to follow them through the locked gates of my mind, through the tangled underbrush and shadows of my own psyche.

To sum up, I replayed, with the priests, the sequence of the process since the first imagined 'moment of disgrace' I had experienced at their hands. What I originally thought were growling, threatening and destructive forces within me, I could now see, once their true essences were revealed, as precious envoys of God, sent in answer to my heart's desires and prayers, to light my path to the freedom I had always longed for. My new freedom, I figured, had to do with an awareness of my dependence on the approval of others for my self-esteem, on a lack of confidence in my own God-given talents, on my need for more guts and courage. (This scenario, in turn, I could begin to see, was but one bead on a string that went all the way back to childhood. That unnoticed string of dependencies and self-worth needs had remained substantially unchanged in over half a century! See *Breathers* Twenty Four and Twenty Five.) Already this awareness was a huge relief that I experienced as pure grace.

What follows in this prolonged *Breather* will try to indicate how this entire process served to set the foundations for a more mature and pure way of serving others. But, for the moment, let me mention again the main disclosure-moment in all of this – how truly interesting it is that now, after first sitting unjudgementally in the empty clearing of the forest of my mind and feelings, I was once again re-naming my erstwhile beasts of prey – my negative, distressing reactions – not as enemies anymore, but as beloved companions of my soul, called compassion, love, courage, service.

To separate so as to hold
The above example endeavours to give a quick glance at the speeded-up unfolding of the process of transforming the negative. It is a very special skill where nature and grace work together. I even think that it is at the heart of Christ's passover and of our own participation in it. For that reason it is worth retracing the steps and examining the sequence of the process more fully. It is important to remember that, by holding it in patience, the negative or hurting emotion in question may turn out to be quite different from the first diagnosis. It is as we wait for the layers of surface meanings to be replaced by more authentic ones, that much essential disclosure takes place. This exercise of holding and 'breathing into' the jealousy or fear or shame is the surest place for transformation to happen. It can be a mistake, as we saw in the above example, to name the emotion too definitively too soon. We close the door on vital, personal discovery whenever we are too sure of our conclusions. What at first feels like the energy of anger, when held for a time of non-judgement, may re-gather itself under a more accurately named emotion. When this kind of self-awareness is happening, true revelation is taking place. But, as with all God's ways with us, especially in the incarnate revelation that was Jesus, this graced moment, too, makes a bloody entrance.

Sometimes, however, the potentially hurtful encounters can be easily transcended. With practice, the negative reaction or emotional charge resulting from many everyday comments, silences and body-language, can be swiftly absorbed, or even ignored. Quite often I suggest to myself that I simply don't have the time or the energy just now to make an issue of this or that possible 'put-down' or criticism. More and more often, these days, I cannot be bothered with trying to figure out the reasons for people's motives or my own reactions. I just let it go, sometimes almost immediately, and get on with my life.

However, when the 'heavy-duty stuff' happens, I have to attend more carefully to how I am present to the experience. What is important is not to retaliate unthinkingly on the one hand or, on the other, to retreat behind an angry, silent sulk. My body is deeply and visibly affected by both of these reactions. Neither is it a true response, although often a laudable one, to 'grin and bear it' until you have time to rationalise the whole incident, (as I often do). This only results in 'explaining away' the event by weaving a story around it, by supplying all kinds of possible reasons for the other person's 'attack', by enlisting the support of sympathetic friends to justify your own sense of being an innocent victim. Once you prove the other person to be wrong, you automatically assume yourself to be right, needing no further self-exploration or inner awareness. (On a broader canvas, this terrible self-righteous justification is a classic ploy of churches and states to exploit and control public opinion about, for instance, the maintaining of some kind of moral superiority or the justification of certain wars.)

None of these three reactions or responses will lead to your own personal growth. None of them are truly authentic. A fertile potential moment of inner knowledge and wisdom is lost. You end up, after a brief and false feeling of satisfaction, either feeling diminished or back where you were. What is recommended by the wise ones we trust is to simply 'sit with' the feeling without explaining, vindicating or blaming. 'Breathe into it.' Stay with the breathing. Allow the connected thoughts, memories or feelings back to your meditation for as long as it takes. Do not wish or force them away. This only puffs them up. Neither should you feed or empower them, by wrestling with them, denying or distorting them. Have no expectations. Just calmly continue to observe, as though at a distance, all that is taking place in your head, heart and body (see *Breather* Two). The anxieties, fears or resentments will return again and again, to knock on your door, to repossess your house; you do not have to invite them in. Neither do you argue. You keep your peace and courteously respect the distance between you and them.

To hold so as to understand
Sometimes I imagine myself sitting in a clearing in the forest. I am quite still, waiting for what may emerge from the dark places between the trees around me. It is not a comfortable place to be. It requires courage and confidence to face the empty void. What will appear? It may be a ferocious dragon; it may be a playful rabbit. Richard Rohr calls this time of non-judging a threshold moment, a paradigm shift, the holding of life-giving and death-dealing opposites in the centre of our soul. This threshold-time of holding or sitting with the disturbing feeling, is about giving life a chance to teach us something new and maybe very necessary for our inward growth. As already mentioned, we may have named and labelled the initial emotion too soon and too negatively. So as to understand and accept something of the mystery of our lives, it may be better to withhold any final naming for some time. Other hidden issues in our life-stories may be carefully masked. The shadow lives well below the surface. There may be much more to this seemingly obvious emotion and our immediate response, than we suspect. The fisherman may be unaware that the slight drag on the line could be indicating a big catch, down below and out of sight. It is time for a rare patience. To escape from the pain too soon is to miss the inbuilt possibility for healing and growing, waiting to reveal itself. At this point, we now move on to another significant opportunity for growth in grace to become available.

We need to learn to live with ambiguity. Rohr has much to offer about the blessing it is, to be able to hold together the opposites in our lives. In a desert-ranch in Abiquiu, New Mexico, under a huge picture of the naked, crucified Christ, arms outstretched between oppression and freedom, between pain and joy, between night and day, he reminded us of the role of holding ambiguity and the conflict of differences in our own lives too. The arms of our fleshed souls are extended between the good and bad thieves of our own spirit and environment, between the dreams of our hearts and the reality of our days, between the fine passions of our spirit and the flawed passions of our sinfulness. Somewhere along the time of our lives we have been led to believe that things should be otherwise, that our days ought to be lived out beneath a cloudless sky! Somewhere inside us we expect our existence to be always happy, that unhappiness is a foreign body to be neutralised and excluded as totally and finally as possible. Reality, however, is different. Nobody promised us an everlasting rose-garden. And even the rose-garden contains weeds and flowers. Getting rid of the weeds may damage the roses. Let them all grow together, said Jesus, the wheat and the tares. A healthy garden can hold them all. There is a night and a day in every twenty-four hours. There is a dark side to every ray of light. Each moment of joy has its suffering twin. This is always the way it will be. It is the way it is. There is a world of wisdom in the acceptance of this truth. The way it is.

Even while writing this *Breather*, and therefore being sensitive to the wiles and subtleties of the ego, I walked, unheedingly, right into a situation where my pride took a sharp beating. The difference between my expectations of my contribution in a certain instance, and the reality of the situation as perceived by another, was a shock to my system. I felt unvalued and worthless. It was an extraordinary moment, and only with the help of some friends, afterwards, did I recognise it as pure gift, as an answer to prayer, as the very raw material of transformation – the substance of this *Breather*. As I 'sat in the clearing', so to speak, having put some distance between my true self and the angry ego, I began to see the encounter as a small experience of the emptying of my false self, of the dying to my proud ego. How else could I have been purified a little more, liberated another tiny bit from my dependence on my own achievements, thrown back into the arms of God as my only reality? I could now see that when the commitment is made to the inner journey, nothing happens by chance. Everything belongs. The way it is, is perfect. *Tout est grace.*

I realised that when this transition was taking place within me, I was participating, according to God's will, in what Jesus first did on the cross. I was continuing in my own body, the crucifixion of Christ. In the holding, within my heart, of these seemingly opposite positions – my puffed-up dream of myself and the harsh reality of who I really am – I was experiencing both death and resurrection. When I received Holy Communion the following morning, and as the body and blood of Jesus was transformed so intimately into the very substance of my own body, I realised more clearly some of the profound meaning of our sacred participation in the suffering, death and resurrection of Jesus. Each time that this passover is enacted in our lives, we are set free to love a little more – a little more strongly and a little more carefully. And so is the whole world. In his Letter to the Ephesians, St Paul has a powerful passage:

> For Jesus is the peace between us, and has made the two into one and broken down the barrier which used to keep them apart, actually destroying in his own person the hostility caused by the rules and decrees of the Law. This was to create one single New Man in himself out of the two of them and by restoring peace through the cross, to unite them both in a single Body and reconcile them with God. In his own person he killed the hostility . . . You are all part of God's household. You are part of a building that has the apostles and prophets for its main corner-stone. As every structure is aligned on him, all grow into one holy temple in the Lord; and you too, in him, are being built into a house where God lives, in the Spirit. (2:14-22)

That, I think, is what we try to do with the contrasting inhabitants of our hearts. We hold them trustingly. This is immensely difficult to do. Such trust does not come easily or cheaply. It is a scary time. We are so often utterly confused by the antics, posturings and protestations of the sub-personalities of our psychic make-up. There is, for instance, no end to the sheer and subtle power of the ego that, at its most destructive, can totally distort the nature of reality (see *Breather* Three). Neither is there any limit to the surge of pure energy and vision that makes us feel only a little less than the angels. We are, indeed, at the mercy of great and elemental forces that stem from the unfathomable mystery of our infancy – an infancy that is to be measured, not in decades, but in the centuries and millennia that sometimes rage and sometimes sing just below the surface of our ordinary-day thoughts and feelings. There is a sense in which we are ultimately helpless before the inexorable and relentless destiny of life. In a soon-to-be-published poem, *The Letter*, Angela Hanley wrote:

> I want to hold your hand,
> cradle your head and whisper;

you are all of your past –
the pain and the betrayal belong;
embrace all of it, see its place
in your history, root it in its time,
salute it, leave it be and travel on
knowing it is the other side of love.

Thus it was with Jesus. There are no shades or subtleties of personal or archetypal shadow that he did not encounter at extreme levels in this often-tormented soul. Holding the opposites together did not come easy for him. In his forty desert days he was wracked by his violent demons. He was no stranger to the painful ambiguity of his reconciling mission. Nor did he endure the self-destroying role of peacemaker with unflinching stoicism and white-knuckle fixity of purpose. In his all-too-human efforts to contain the paradox of uncertainties he absorbed one, then the other; he held them both lightly; flexible between contradictory positions, he moved with faith between them, never too sure of the nature of the mystery that was unfolding within him. In the midst of his night of holding on to the extremes he was destined from all time to carry, while devastated and despairing, he was obedient. He listened to the whisper of his divine Parent even when it faded into total silence. Jesus struggled, but not too violently and not for too long. He, too, knew it was the other side of love.

Like Jesus, we also try to struggle free but such struggle does not bring freedom. The freedom we long for does not come at the end of a definitive war against whatever makes us insecure, uncertain or unhappy. True freedom lies in the way we stand before the unknown, the unpredictable, 'the enemy'. We stand before whatever seems to be threatening us, confusing us, hurting us, robbing us of our peace, not with the glare of resentment, anger or hatred in our eyes, but with the gaze of compassion in our hearts. Even though this condition of pure presence takes a lifetime's journey, it is the only way to be before the mystery of pain and the paradox of light and darkness. We learn to reconcile the contradictions, the unfinishedness, the despairing, the diminishing routine, the less than perfect in our lives. The anxious effort to escape, to be defensive, to be cautious, to resist, only intensifies the suffering and alienation. Approaching this most important dimension of our inward journey from a different but related angle, Alan Watts, in *The Wisdom of Insecurity* writes:

The pain is inescapable, and resistance as a defence only makes it worse; the whole system is jarred by the shock. Running away from fear is fear, fighting pain is pain, trying to be brave is being scared. Seeing that there is no escape from the pain, the mind yields to it, absorbs it, and becomes conscious of just pain . . . Pain is the nature of this present moment, and I can only live in this moment. Pain and the effort to be separate from it are the same thing. Wanting to get out of pain is the pain. When you discover this, the desire to escape merges into the pain itself and vanishes. All of this is not an experiment, a trick, to be held in reserve for a moment of crisis. It is a way of life. It means being aware, alert and sensitive to the present moment always, in all actions and relationships whatsoever, beginning at this instant. . . Here life is alive, vibrant, vivid and present, containing depths which we have scarcely begun to explore. (pp 88, 89)

Let me attempt a partial summary. When we try to overcome emotional pain and suffering, we often believe that if we avoid or ignore it, then in some way it will disappear, that it will go away and stop hurting. What we discover is that this type of resistance to facing the issue can often have the reverse effect by intensifying the distress, leaving us numb and immobilised at best or, at worst, leading us to project our pain and negative reactions on to others.

When we reflect on the image of the cross, we see Jesus writhing in his agony, physically nailed to his anguish, restrained and restricted by the conditions that have the power to end his journey and his life. He cannot avoid this awful place – but trapped though he is, he is still free to choose. He can chose to be disempowered by allowing the hurting and grief within him to turn outwards as an expression of bitterness, aiming to deflect away from himself the pangs of pain by blaming, indicting and condemning those who set out to destroy all that his holy heart had longed for. Instead, he waits. He holds the disfiguring torments within himself by simply accepting it – accepting it without judgement, falling back into the arms of the One whose width and depth, whose height and length, surpasses all created understanding. It is from this waiting-space of inner holding that the one response of Jesus is created – the powerful out-flowing of unconditional love. His pain is still pain, his death on the cross is still a stark and deadly sin, but by accepting without resisting, by trusting in a mystery that transcends the awful horror of that moment, his death-filled agony is trans-formed into a life-giving energy – the beginning of resurrection.

When we resist the positive ways of encountering the dimin-ishing and debilitating forces, while experiencing a temporary pseudo-relief or satisfaction, we succeed only in sinking into a swampy, immobilising place that prevents any movements of healing or towards freedom and light. But if, like Jesus, we can accept all, even though we may well feel that we do not under-stand anything; if we can trust enough to wait and hold the painful memories and emotions within us even though some-thing inside us is crying out for revenge or retaliation – then, and only then, a blessed peace, a greater understanding and a deeper insight into the meaning within the dark feelings is released within us – revealing the way through, into the growing, loving spaces of our liberated souls. That is the moment when we truly know that Jesus Christ is raised from the dead.

To understand so as to love
There is a need for most of us to learn again the language and dynamics of what is now called 'process'. Process has to do with interdependence and mutuality. It is not about the cut-and-dried, handed-down certainties of the past or about the free-for-all, sheer individualism that is so prevalent in these post-modern times. In a straight line, and alone, nobody goes very far. There is 'give and take' in process. It is not neat, even and predictable. It is surprising, untidy and sometimes paradoxical. Christian life is about process. This process is not about how to achieve instant happiness, how to end our pain, how to resolve our confusion. It is about how to embrace and hold it, as Jesus did, so as to break-through into the abundant life. The role of the crucified follower of Jesus is to hold together and to reconcile the seeming oppos-ites of gift and shadow, of sin and grace, of light and dark; to be a *pontifex* (a bridge-builder) between 'the good that I would' and 'the evil that I do' (St Paul); to be a reconciler between the negative experiences of my days and the graced nature of my redeemed heart; to be an absorber of the evil in the world rather than to redistribute it in another, and perhaps more subtle shape (see *Breather* Seventeen).

Otherwise we will always carry an unacknowledged split inside us; our psyches will be unable to bear the burden of a contradictory alienation at our centre; we will be a destructively-divided self. And what is also shockingly true is that what is not transformed within us will be transmitted outside us. Unable to reconcile the shadow at our own centre, we scapegoat and demonise all and sundry. Despite all spiritual guidance and psychological theories, as long as we fight against, flee from, deny or explain away the seemingly opposed powers in the mystery of our beings, our truest essence can never be healed within, or empowered to heal the world. In our frantic desperation to rid ourselves of what we perceive as our devils, our angels, too, as the poet Rainer Maria Rilke warned us, may take flight.

The only end of this holy process is to increase the love in the world by humbly holding, and then transforming the hateful and the hurtful. It is not easy to refrain from judging. When we judge we recklessly project our own blindness. To be non-judgemental is to be saved. From the raw material of the negative and fallen bits of each day's experiences, by virtue of our birth and baptism, we are called to be alchemists of love. This is the painful ego-death from which the summer blossoms grow. This is the winter-holding where, all out of sight, the transforming miracles happen. It is the travelling with Jesus from our own Good Fridays to our Easter Sundays. It is our co-saving of the world with him, our co-creating of a new springtime for the churches. 'I, if I be lifted up, will draw all things to myself.'

In summary, the energy that initially draws us out on our inner journey of destiny, that sensitises our awareness to the sudden reactions that engulf us, that then enables us to distance ourselves momentarily from those emotions so as to accept and hold them within our hearts, is the human-divine love of God. And the energy that then reconciles the irreconcilable, that builds the bridges across the hostile spaces in between, that holds together the seeming opposites both within ourselves and outside, that breaks down the fear of difference and breaks through into the light, that drives creation relentlessly onwards towards total intimacy with Being itself, is none other than the same uniting, incarnate, divine love that dwells in the heart of all things.

On this journey of the soul, daily there will be false hopes, disappointments, much self-doubt, loss of nerve, impatience, humiliation and increasingly subtle counter-attacks from the ego. Hold your peace. In the thick of the battles keep your heart at the lotus-feet of the Lord. In God's timing, the light will come. We have an urgent desire for the immediate result, the instant resolution. But very often there is no answer. The answer, as in the journey of Job, is that we do not really need an answer. God has the answer. God understands. And God is holding us. That is more than enough. God is the answer. To each of our questions, the answer is God's own self. In all of this, we are not without a role-model. Jesus himself painfully grew to understand that all of this is the work of a lifetime; but it can be unforgettably glimpsed in one shining moment. In the meantime, the world keeps turning. And the sun continues to shine. And your heart still beats. Then, one of these mornings, you will wake up like a child with a new look in her eyes. And you will find yourself smiling.

Praxis 31

Call in your angels now, as you begin this challenging meditation. Make the Sign of the Cross in honour of the Blessed
Trinity dwelling within you. Light a candle and settle yourself
into your favourite position. Imagine yourself in a thick forest.
You are sitting in the middle of a clearing. Bring your whole self
to this place – your forest of current fears, doubts and longings.
You want to understand what is going on in your life. You have
come here, in the clearing of your soul, to wait for some revelation – a kind of personal vision-quest. You do not know what
will come out from the forest into the clearing. Will it be something threatening? Or will it be gift? You sit and wait. You do not
judge or make any assumptions. After a while you become
aware of something emerging from the shadows. It draws closer.
You are tempted to name it, you want to define it. Do not do so.
Just become aware of it. Continue to sit there and wait. Let it
continue to reveal itself. Breathe into the unnamed emotion that
is still surfacing. Remain with this conscious 'breathing into'.
Some insight or self-knowledge or piece of wisdom will disclose
itself enough to be recognised and held. Now, again, you become conscious of your surroundings in the forest. You are
alone in the clearing. Gently ask yourself 'What was it that
emerged from the forest? What did I learn? What enlightenment, what gift did it bring? How can I internalise that revelation into my very being and consciousness? How would I name
it now?' Are you at peace? Or are you more distressed? Can you
see the gift in whatever happened in the clearing? Even though
what was revealed to you may bring a new distress, can you believe that this revelation, too, is a grace? Do you feel that you can
hold all these glimpses about yourself in calmness, even as you
believe yourself to be held by your ever-loving God?

Nota Bene:
You are called to be authentic, not perfect

It is difficult to travel light when burdened with the goal of perfection. On a journey where risk, letting go and openness are the only spiritual compasses to hand, the attainment of perfection is a dubious destination. When much of the ground is covered by night, with the stars as the only guides and the Holy Spirit on a wild, confusing rampage among the shadows of the mind, it is extremely foolish to persist in holding on to a pre-determined address. However it is peddled by the shopkeepers of God and Mammon, perfection does not consist in the secure possession of the 'state of grace', the perfectly balanced mind or the finely-tuned, tanned body. We are led astray by the holy allurements of perfect integration, total harmony and 'having it all together' just as surely as by the false attractions of the devil. We have survived the seduction of the 'body-beautiful' image only to spiritualise the same materialistic narcissism into the equally deadly trap of the 'soul-beautiful' image. We are betrayed by both images. In their blind and urgent immediacy, they twist our bodies and souls out of true. Because all we can ever hope to be is *authentic*.

That is why self-awareness, to be present to each moment, is about as far as we can go. Whatever way we are, that is the way we are. When we sin, we sin. When we get it right, we get it right. When we are off balance and excessive, we are off balance and excessive. Such are the shapes, the colours and contours of authenticity. Balanced perfection happens only at the infinite horizon, God's other home, from where the panoramic view of how it all fits together is clear. Close up, however, our lives have no option but to be unbalanced, in disorder and incomplete – like one note from Pachelbel's *Canon in D;* like one word from a Shakespeare sonnet; like one moment from *Swan Lake.*

How else could we hop precariously from stone to stone across the river of wisdom on the way home, or let go and risk finding the lifeline of hands that draw and release us onwards, or believe that the half-understood, unfinished whispers we hear belong to God? Against the background of ultimate perfection, we must always be losing our own balance. Without such a loss, not even the tiniest step could be taken – a condition of *rigor mortis* would prevail. Usually we are only truly authentic (and therefore perfect) when we know we are lost. In the context of the mystery of salvation, it is the safest place to be.

It was a dull, flat, February morning. Susan, the teacher, had gathered the reception-class around me. We had just watched the acting-out of the Parable of the Lost Sheep in the school hall. Now, back in the classroom, they were telling me, in turn, why they had chosen the various parts they played – the ninety-nine who stayed secure in the sheep-fold, the brave shepherds who went out searching, the readers of the parable, and so on. Finally it was Laura's turn, the little girl who had volunteered to play the part of the lost sheep. 'I wanted to be lost,' she said with a small smile, 'so that somebody would come and find me.'

PART THREE

At a New Threshold

You have been invited to meet the Friend.
No one can resist a Divine Invitation.
That narrows down all your choices
To just two:

We can come to God
Dressed for Dancing
Or
Be carried on a stretcher
To God's Ward.
(Hafiz)

High Noon at Ghost Ranch
A message from the desert

What sustains us during the morning of life,' wrote Carl Jung, 'will not see us through the afternoon.' It is high noon during the mid-life years. It is a time of transition. Almost one hundred men, aged between twenty and seventy, gathered in the high desert of northern New Mexico, to experience a breakthrough in our lives. Packed into bunks in the scorching heat and sharing everything, a picnic it was not! The four days with Richard Rohr, a well-known Franciscan priest, were all about the male spiritual journey, about the passages that mark the decades of our lives and about how to negotiate them. I won't forget those days in a hurry!

Some two hundred million years of earth history are exposed at Ghost Ranch. The landscape is vast and other-worldly in its beauty. Geographically, this small oasis lies in the heart of the Chama River which links the Colorado Plateau with the Rio Grande Valley. I'm writing these reflections a few days later, at the Madonna Centre, sixty miles south, in Albuquerque. And, outside my window, the Rio Grande, carrying all kinds of magic memories of cowboy songs from my childhood, is flowing towards El Paso, and then on to the Gulf of Mexico.

What happens during the high noon of which I write is a difficult experience. It is about moving on into another landscape of our lives with new horizons and perspectives. It is about going through a door from one room in our soul to the next, in a most definitive and committed way. I can only describe it as a kind of baptism and rebirth, a rite of passage that is for real. Men in general do not find it easy; for the priests who were there, it was a frightening challenge. The experience of marriage and of family has a way of maturing a person; many of us priests stay stuck in a never-ending adolescence.

Rite of male initiation

At Ghost Ranch we were challenged to let go of the egocentric structures of the earlier decades of our lives – the preoccupations with image and success, with ambition and achievement, with reputation and competition. This involves a painful death, a sacrifice of the false self to regain the freedom of the true self. This, when entered into in depth, is the fundamental passover, the primordial conversion in the living out of our Christian baptism and priesthood. And words and prayers are not enough to disentangle, explore and transform, in a few days, what has been planted, rooted and inseparably intertwined in our very way of being, for many decades.

Most of our desert days were about getting in touch with and expressing such deep-seated feelings and buried memories. At high noon on a Sunday, with only precious water to drink, we walked apprehensively out among the burning rocks and the hidden snakes, to find a remote place away from others, to draw our circle around us in the stinging sand, and to sit for hours within it, as aware of God's voice as possible, but without deliberate thinking or planning. During those days, too, we fasted and chanted, we immersed ourselves in a sacred pool, we re-enacted many primitive practices and we beat incessantly on our drums. We confessed our sins and affirmed each other. We told our secrets and wept openly. We marked the wounded parts of our bodies with mercurichrome. We danced around a campfire and hugged each other in sorrow and in joy. We were deeply moved by the stark and powerful imagery of the morning rituals. It was playful; it was deadly serious. It was truly sacramental in a way I had never experienced before. And it all happened in public.

We were a mixed bunch. There were lawyers and doctors, judges and executives, priests and students. I gathered this only through small group sharing, because outwardly, there were no ranks or class distinctions. We all wore the same outfit – jeans and black or white T-shirts depending on the theme of the day. Stripped of all distinguishing marks, what we had in common was our maleness. And, of course, our struggle. It was a sweaty, bloody, primitive *metanoia*, a raw ritual of searing honesty, a naked encounter with the shattered dimensions of our own empty lives and those of our brothers. I could feel in my body the reconciliation happening within and around me, the breakthrough from the traps of time and memory into 'the new man', the blessed release from the meaningless and disillusionment of mid-life (35-55) into the contentment of being the 'wise old fool', the holy grandfather, or whatever term from the legendary Hero's Journey had most meaning for us.

As I sat and listened to Richard's compassionate reflections, and to those other vulnerable men as they told their truth, my tears were flowing. What were those tears about, I wondered? Were they tears for myself, at the pain of this inner journey, of this shedding of my many masks, of this relentless pursuit of my own humanity? Were they tears of loss and grief, over the false and mistáken sacrifice of compulsory celibacy in a disintegrating church? This was some kind of personal crucifixion that stretched me between my essential humanity, on the one outstretched hand and, on the other, the priesthood I had acquired. Does the clericalism of our institutional church really destroy our true identity so much? Devoid of family – God's natural way of rounding people off, of breaking down the pretentious and touchy edges of our personalities, of balancing out our selfish, childish wilfulness – how many of us see ourselves as unwilling victims of our enforced celibacy? Or is it just me?

The inscrutable priest

I'm wondering, as I write this, what other priests would say. Would they be glad that they themselves are so fulfilled and happy in their work, and then simply dismiss me as a crank, a loner, who should stop belly-aching about these matters and get on with his prayers? Oddly enough I'm not unhappy. I am very optimistic about the future, I feel a real fulfilment in my vocation and I experience a very deep loving in my life. But I'm also trying to be authentic, truthful and realistic about what is currently happening in my own 'one, wild and precious life' and also in the lives of my brother priests these decades. I have noticed that women do not ridicule each other when they try to expose and share the losses and longings of their hearts and bodies. Rather they affirm each other tenderly and hold each other compassionately while this inner journey is travelled.

Fresh from the truthfulness of Ghost Ranch, I ask whether other priests feel no great loss, no deprivation of an essential dimension of being a full human being, no sense of being deluded by an unrepentant institution. I don't suppose we'll ever know.

To do so would be to break ranks, to be disloyal. We are all so inscrutable. We reveal so little. We find it hard to trust. To confess to weakness is unthinkable. To be vulnerable is to have failed. That is why we hate admitting to being lost, sad or overlooked. But the men at Ghost Ranch cried out, over and over again, a litany of the hurts and abuses that they themselves had suffered and had caused others to suffer. They wept, shouted, whispered, choking on the words as they uttered them aloud for the first time in their lives.

In my experience of giving retreats to priests I have rarely come across such heartfelt emotional release. Yet of all people, we need it most. What have we done with our anger and grief? They are either seething inside us like cast-iron pressure-cookers or, perhaps, we no longer feel anything much anymore. Either way the passion for the possible is lost. I have met priests and bishops who, with broken hearts, have fearfully shared about their loss of faith in God and in the efficacy of the sacraments they celebrate and of the prayers they publicly lead. This 'dark night of the soul' is a terrible kind of dying. These are the ones who are being tried by fire, whose spirituality is being purified in the most ultimate way. However, in public, most priests seem quite sure about how happy they are. Now that most of us are over fifty, maybe this insistence is because the chances of promotion have vanished, the prospect of early retirement seems ever more attractive, the temptations of the flesh are burning low and, after all, haven't we a good house with all the mod cons, someone to look after us, freedom from financial worries, and still lots of prestige and status.

Shapes of the cross
The physical backdrop of all that happened in the hall at Ghost Ranch this summer was Stephen Gambill's new and striking picture of the naked, crucified Christ, holding, within his own body the tensions and paradoxes, the irreconcilable aspects of his own life, of the lives of each one of us and of the unfolding of all creation. To be a reconciler like this, as we are called to be, is almost humanly impossible. Yet that is what those men in the desert were striving to achieve – to be alchemists of humanity, transforming, in their hearts, minds and bodies, their own sins and the sins of their 'enemies'. The true man within us, we were told, the 'hero', the 'wild man', is the one who walks his journey

into wholeness and holiness, integrating the paradoxical aspects of his nature and vocation. He does not need to dominate others and has transcended his hidden fear of women. He knows that every pain he refuses to absorb into his own self will be projected and transmitted on to others with dreadful consequences.

All of this is no more or no less than the living out of our baptism in the womb/tomb dimensions of every moment of growth, and of the daily experiencing of the life/death passover of our Saviour. But can we accept the inner contradictions of trying to live the Christian life in our flawed and conditioned humanity? On the one hand there is the desire to control, to fix and to judge with the calculating mind; on the other hand, there is the way of surrender, of letting go, of trusting, of living in the present moment with the contemplative mind. The heart of the priest is the bloody battleground where the necessary encounter between his devils and his angels take place; it is the playground, too, where light and shadow must forever dance. As priests we can only name and call forth the demons in others that we are already familiar with within ourselves; we can only be authentic with others to the extent that we are authentic with ourselves; we can only walk responsibly with others as far as the limits of our own inner journey; we can only share the graces that we have first embodied; we can only give away that gold which we have first made our own.

Otherwise the mid-life and older priest runs the risk of becoming useless, of never truly knowing himself, of settling for a passionless routine, of closing up his emotions and closing down his energy, of hiding his sad pain in well-known ways of denial, and of becoming 'the embittered old fool' depicted in the classic legends of the human quest. There are many of us in this category, at least for some of the time. The process for men, because men are as much oppressed by the system as women are, is about first recognising our grief, and then about expressing it, absorbing it, holding it (like the figure on the cross) without blaming or scapegoating. Because grief is unfinished hurt, and because it lies under the stone of anger, how hard this is to do! Small wonder that we so desperately resist the call to examine the invisible and powerful compulsions that rage, like underground torrents, beneath our daily decisions and motivations, influencing and controlling us to a degree we could never believe.

The tears of things

This holding of our pain and hurt and that of others, without anger or retaliation, is a kind of calvary, a personal crucifixion, a profound encounter with the lacrimae rerum. There are palaces, it says in the Zohar, that open only to tears. This awareness of the distance between what we preach, and who we really are, does not bear facing up to. This living with the ambiguity of our lives, and with the paradox of things, is impossible without knowing that we are somehow unconditionally loved. Even then we struggle with our helplessness and powerlessness. No matter what, we cannot engineer our own transformation. We find it so hard to believe that our salvation is not brought about by 'being good' or by 'getting it right' but by being connected with God; not by not sinning but by intimacy with our Creator-Lover; not by wearing the proud badges of our public image, but by approaching each other, in reverent humility and bare-foot, over the shattered vases of our broken vows; not by de-spairing at the fractured and contradictory nature of the aspira-tions of our hearts, but by rejoicing that somehow, somewhere, 'everything belongs' and is safely harvested in the barns of eter-nity. At the end of the day, and of our lives, it is not so much about religion as about relationship.

As the long, sharp days at Ghost Ranch jolted by, we gradu-ally began to accept more totally our condition of mortality, but believing too, that somehow or other, we grow younger as we grow older in our daily dying to self. We began to realise that our 'inner despair' (Rahner) and our 'quiet desperation' (Thoreau), when identified, accepted and expressed, will not lead us to an opting out, a breaking down, a deeper depression or addiction, or suicide. When integrated into our truest human-ity or, as all priests know, when united with the passion of Jesus Christ, this despair and desperation will be redeemed and will empower us with the healing graces and transforming blessings of God. All our wounds will become sacred wounds. It is not about giving up, giving in, or about a defeated submission. It is, ultimately, about the strength of surrender, the blind and wild leap of faith into the unfathomable mystery of Love.

A man's two journeys

Like most men, priests like to play the role of the 'man's man', independent, in control, a decisive authority and a hard worker.

Yet behind this image of power and status there is, we were told at Ghost Ranch, much insecurity, immaturity and a well-disguised anxiety. There is a fear that springs from the unconscious understanding of our own ultimate insignificance and mortality; a fear that we have somehow lost our individuality, sold out on our humanity and become dry and superficial. Whether the 'oppressing system' is seen in terms of political pressure, profit targets or religious allegiance and conformity, most men do not regard themselves as victims. While so many women are on the path of liberation, most men are unaware of the shallowness of their lives, of how cut off they are from the centres of their being, and of how they need to be saved from the establishments that castrate them of their creative powers. Priests who do not know what to do with their pain will almost certainly abuse their power.

The first journey, according to Richard Rohr, that a man must take out of his unexplored masculinity is that of John the Beloved, with whom Jesus had a special intimacy, and who was not afraid to lean on his friend's breast at the Last Supper. This is an inward journey into the feminine part of a man's psyche, but it is heavily formed by the significant women a man encounters in life – his mother, sisters, girlfriends, wife. At a time in the seventies, when priests seemed more confused than usual, it was my own relationships, I believe, that kept me human and vulnerable, open, trusting and receptive. There were many hurts and misunderstandings, and there still are. But I was encouraged to be honest and responsible rather than unaccountable, to stay with the difficulties and find a way through rather than to disappear, to be more sensitive and more nurturing, rather than feeling fearful and guilty about such intimacy.

Eventually, however, if a man does not incorporate the first journey with the second more directional one, he gets stuck in a shallow softness lacking in power and strength. Without focus, determination and self-confidence he lacks the inner authority to move out of his nurturing circle, to direct and drive his own life and the lives of others, particularly if he is ministering as a pastor does. This second journey into the deep masculine is modelled on that made by another who emerged from the desert, John the Baptist. To the first necessary adventure, an additional complementary spiritual energy is enfleshed. This is a new integration of the *animus* and the *anima*, a spirit-filled and empowering inner balance that gives birth to a renewed self. The priest on his second journey does not depend on the latest *ad clerum* for his certainty – he preaches the truth in his own heart without fear or favour – the truth that has set him free. He knows instinctively when lesser rubrics must be disregarded, when secondary commandments must be broken, because a greater need exists.

There is an authoritative accuracy about his insistent call to sinners because it springs from his long acquaintance with the broken beauty of his own soul. He speaks without fear because no one has power over him any more; his whole being and becoming, his working and resting, his praying and sinning are now in time and tune only with God's heartbeat. Nothing else matters. The intimacy and energy that comes from the acknowledgement and sharing of his wound, makes his wound holy, and thus, like Christ's, his anchor. He is now a wounded healer and his power is contagious. The knowledge that he is on the high road to further wounds, failures and to some form of death, only convinces him that he is, finally, on his Lord and Lover's path – the *via dolorosa* to the abundant life both here and in the hereafter.

Message from the desert
Before our initiation was completed, we were given five life-principles to be reflected upon within our circle of sand. These sobering reminders, which were later set into the context of scriptural affirmation and hope, would be written across our hearts for a long time. I recall them here in their desert starkness. The first was a reminder that life is hard. The Initiate must know this in his belly, mind and heart. He must not waste time trying to make life easy for himself. The second makes clear that you are going to die. The mortality and impermanence of your own life must become very real to you. Third, after all, you are not that important. Humility is of central significance for human truth and happiness. All else is window-dressing. In the fourth place, the desert reminded us that you are not in control. You must experience your own powerlessness before a true spiritual journey can begin. And finally, your life is not about you. You are about Life! Your job is to listen, obey and adore, not to calculate, manage and manipulate your own small life or the lives of others.

When these hard messages are internalised, when the two
challenging journeys are embarked upon, when the demanding
Rite of Initiation is duly celebrated, what do we go out into the
desert to find? A man, I tell you; a mature man who is capable of
holding within himself the tension of the paradoxes of life. He
knows that the greater the soul, the greater the shadow. He does
not require certainty but can live with unknowing and mystery.
He does not need to be always 'right', in charge of, or in roles of
command and decision-making. He is ready to empty the cup-
boards of his life of titles, offices and public importance. He
knows who he is, when everything is taken away. He has learned
the hard truth that only his authentic self will live forever. This
radical grace sets him free to act out of his goodness, his essence,
his *anima magna*. Knowing himself to be already divine, his intent is to become truly human, as Jesus still is. He knows, too,
that there is absolutely nothing he can do to make God love him
one bit more, or one bit less. Such is the priest who is free to be
radically compassionate, living beyond judgement, serving
others out of his sacred centre.

He is liberated enough to be care-full and to be care-free because he has surrendered the management of the church and of
the world back into the hands of their Creator. He is free because
he knows that God is greater than any system, denomination or
religion that tries to encompass divine authority and compassion. He is free enough to know that his energies must be spent
in putting obsolete ecclesiastical structures into a new set of
metaphors; into shifting into another paradigm, where the
language and imagery of radical process transforms the static
categories of a current institutionalism which judges and alien-
ates. With this way of being present to mystery, he will never
lose heart, because all his actions, prayers, failures and sins, are
set against what Ronald Rolheiser calls an infinite horizon. This
means that whatever about the immediate outcomes of his life's
efforts, against the infinite horizon of God's acres, nothing is
wasted and everything is harvested.

He is secure enough to be insecure, certain enough of the one
necessary truth to be uncertain about most other matters.
Knowing that rules no longer work in their old form, he abandons
himself to a more reliable and powerful Guide. His shadow is
not just tolerated now; it is forgiven, embraced and seen as gift.
He knows himself to be God's beloved son, the merciful elder

who can hold the paradoxes together because God has 'done this new thing' in him. He is finding, or returning to, a simple wisdom, where to be authentic, transparent and open is more important than to be successful, obeyed or respected. His faith-vision is not about the future. It is about the past – about believing that God has held him every moment of the way up to now, especially in the dead-ends of his journey. So why should he worry about the future? He is travelling light, just breathing and walking. He has no need to plan out the whole itinerary – one, small, trusting step at a time is enough for now. He has nothing, and yet, as Richard said to us on the final day, at the open-air eucharist we celebrated on a canyon-rim of stunning beauty, 'he has it all!'

Riding the Santa Fe Bus
A theological note on 'simply being'

What I'm setting out to do is to show that any attempt at reaching union with God that is based on a deepening awareness of one's own inner being, or of the inner heart of anybody or anything, has a basis in the true meaning of the mystery of creation and of incarnation. This is how I see it. Out of the overwhelming intensity of divine love, God created the world in the first place for companionship. 'God is sheer joy,' taught St Thomas Aquinas, 'and sheer joy demands company.' From that miraculous moment onwards, the world was permeated by God's indwelling love and energy. The Hebrew scriptures make this quite clear. The pre-Christian contemplatives saw God's glory and felt God's presence in everyone and everything. In their silent wonder, the universal, indwelling love and meaning began to become more obvious. The very nature of creation, they began to understand, revealed the nature of God.

In the one person of Jesus, we find the unique and irrevocable meeting between creation's graced openness to divine fulfilment and God's creative and loving desire to achieve this intimacy. In him was completed and perfected the first longing of creation for God and God's own desire to fulfil that longing by becoming eternally united with humanity and creation. In him, the listening ear of a groaning and straining creation heard the divine music it was coded to hear from the beginning – the unceasingly uttered Word of a self-surrendering God. Christ revealed, once-for-all and in his own human self, the 'hidden agenda' of God's initial creation, by being at once 'the way forward' for the final and unrepeatable breakthrough of that creation into God and, at the same time, by being 'the way in' for the ever-approaching, self-disposing, divine emptying of God into the world that God had first conceived out of love.

To live is holy
In his celebrated Jubilee Letter, Pope John Paul engaged with a
theology of creation. As well as telling the mythical tale of
humanity's fall from grace and a subsequent salvation, this rich
understanding of revelation holds that creation and incarnation
can also be read as the greatest lovestory, revealing all of us as
being a delight to God, carefully fashioned in God's image. With
or without a definitive 'fall', God would have longed for an
intimate union with a human being and could not have been
prevented from assuming the beautiful humanity of a man
called Jesus. And it came to pass that the Word became flesh,
and dwelt amongst us. All the hunches that a universal and
divine energy ran through the still centre of everything, sustain-
ing and nurturing growth and evolution of every kind, could
now be completely believed. In Jesus, all the hints, suspicions
and guesses about the God who moved in the inner heart of
things, nourishing and caressing all forms of becoming, were,
once for all, vindicated. From now on, the matter was beyond
discussion – the unquestioned humanity of Jesus Christ was the
living symbol and sacrament of God's assumption of creation as
God's earthly mode of being.

The arrival of Jesus on the stage of life's evolution brought
the drama of God and the world into another Act. God's pure
essence, which is love, is now guaranteed for ever, as being the
source of the life of all living things. Those early Hebrew seers
and prophets who, in their holy stillness, heard the faint, muffled
rhythm of a deeper music, were not mistaken. Their pre-Christian
souls were finely attuned to the divine score, long before it
flowed across the world with its stunning beauty, in the symphony
that was Jesus. I write this to provide a theological rationale for
holding that to live is holy, that to simply be is blessed and that
the condition of awareness is a true form of adoration. This
prayer of awareness is coming from the gurus of the East and
from the poets of the West, from the mystics of the past and the
contemplatives of the present. It is as old as the hills and as new
as a baby. It is not a special kind of awareness about a special
kind of subject. It is any kind of true awareness about any part of
created reality. That is why an intent and focused silence in the
face of this amazing mystery is the main condition for hearing
God's heartbeat in the cacophany of our lives. That is why to
simply be in the presence of the immediate commerce of life is

the closest we can get to worship. The present moment is the real presence of God.

The Albuquerque Inn

At this point in my scribbling I pause to look around me. I stretch and breathe. My body is a little cramped but it feels good. I'm having a pint and a snack here in downtown Albuquerque. The Budweiser tastes weak; the cajun-style chicken is spicy and tasty. It is stifling hot outside; the air-conditioning inside is heaven. A small child's face is all crumpled up with loss and fear – she has just inadvertently burst her red balloon. Her sister offers her own. One grandparent chides her; the other smiles. There's music in the background – country and western songs from the sixties. A murmur of conversation. The telephone rings. A loud laugh draws attention to itself. Another car sweeps into the parking lot. Bright with smiles, energy, mutual adoration and jewelry, two young black people flow out of the car and dance into The Village Inn. The telephone rings again.

I come back to my thoughts. So this is it. If I'm right, here in front of me the true nature of God is being revealed. Right here and right now the paschal mystery is gradually unfolding in all its ordinariness and in all its glory. All I have to do is be present to it – really and truly present to it in a way that sees into the heart of things. This kind of worship is more than a superficial noticing; it is a becoming-one with what happens, and therefore a becoming-one with God. It is the practical implication of what our best catechisms and our current Eucharistic Prayers keep reminding us about, namely, the presence of God everywhere – the God 'in whom we live and move and have our being'. Here around the busy tables of The Village Inn, if we tune in to the amazing mystery of the most ordinary of daily happenings, multiplied by millions of times around the inns of the world, is the living-out of what we did around the eucharistic table last Sunday. This was the celebration of what Jesus revealed in his life, death and resurrection, namely, that God is reaching to me in and between every beat of my heart, every breath I draw, every sound and movement around me, everything that happens, or ever happened, or ever will happen. So, as a human being and a Catholic Christian, what is this theological reflection saying to me then? It is simply saying – Wake up! Don't miss it! Be present to the miracle of the ordinary!

The full revelation of God in the full humanity of Jesus has signalled to the world that, by virtue of Jesus' solidarity with the rest of creation, the rest of creation, too, has the potential to reveal God. Jesus thought with a human mind, loved with a human heart and forgave with a human compassion. It is to the extent that we are true in our human loving, authentic in our presence to our sisters and brothers, aware, compassionate and just in 'right relationship' with the fragile balances of the earth's resources, that God becomes visible and tangible and knowable to us. Whenever, therefore, we are trying to be fully present to our own created essence, or to that of others, or to any created thing, even a drop of water or a grain of sand, that is when we aspire to intimacy with God.

To be is blessed

To be truly present, however, requires persistent awareness, attention, focus, the ability to stay with, to wonder at, to be lost in, to wake up to the holiness of the present moment. That is the reason for the prayer of quiet, for contemplation, for meditation, for the mystical path. That is the reason for celebrating the sacraments, with all those natural elements that remind us of God's energy already flowing through all things. Without a deep awareness of God's healing presence in every aspect of time and space, from the beginning to the end, and in every split-second and split-atom in-between, our celebration of baptism and eucharist can never be authentically sacramental.

In these pages I only want to indicate, with large brush strokes, the fundamental principles for holding that *to simply be* is enough. We can say such a thing with faith and courage because, working backwards and forwards from the revelation that was Jesus, we now know that God is always offering God's own self in every dimension of life. Every created moment and thing is a blessed sacrament of God's real presence. Whenever, for instance, we experience the heartfelt feelings of anyone, we are experiencing God. Whenever we truly love anybody, we save that person forever, because our love is divine. When we forgive somebody, that person is forgiven by God. This is so amazing that most people dismiss it as untrue. It is too simple and too profound. To love anyone truly is to be another Christ, to be God incarnate.

There are not two loves. There is not another 'higher' level of being. To believe otherwise is to be guilty of dualism, to deny the meaning of the incarnation. We want signs and wonders, oblivious to the miracles around us every day. We want priests and scapegoats as 'in-betweens', between ourselves and God and between ourselves and sin and between ourselves and ourselves. We would rather live in a two-tier world, misunderstanding the whole point of the incarnation, pandering to magic and superstition in our dualistic devotions, seeing 'ordinary' life as 'merely' secular and always hankering after the 'sacred' people, sacred places and sacred things in the fruitless search for what is already lying in abundance at our finger-tips. But not so with the fourteenth century Persian poet Hafiz:

One regret, dear world,
That I am determined not to have
When I am lying on my deathbed
Is that
I did not kiss you enough.[41]

Only one love
We forget that the world is the body of God, that, as the poets remember, eternity is caught in the most commonplace moment, infinity in a passing gesture and divinity in every aspiration of the human heart. Without the fact of the enfleshing of the Word, no poet or mystic could hold, with absolute certainty, what the Hebrew authors glimpsed – that every drop of water, every grain of sand, every leaf, every feeling were all small sacraments of divinity. So important and holy is the 'being' of things, the 'isness' of things, the life-breath of any creature, the heartbeat of the tiniest insect, that to become one with it, is to become one with God. Once again, we listen to the mystic-author of *The Cloud of Unknowing*: 'If you look at God in the perspective of eternity,' he writes, 'there is no name you can give him – nor is there any experience or understanding – which is more fitting that that which is contained in the blind and lovely beholding of the word *is*.' Above all, when we struggle to love as truly as we can, then, especially, is when we are held in mystery. (Mystery being the context and unfathomable backdrop, the infinite horizon to all our human searching and loving.) So when we stop thinking distracting thoughts, when we are attentive to the present moment and to all that is going on all around us, when we trust in the 'now', letting go of everything that is not in that

'now', then, to my mind, we are sensing the liberating reality of God.

The mystics describe this kind of attention as something like the way people in love gaze in silence at each other and are privileged to enter some reserved inner *sanctum*, out of bounds to all but the lover. When people are gifted with this mutual loving, there is a deeper mystery present. The revelation of the incarnation is not about a third element in this relationship, as though God's love was another dimension to be included in the equation. Any form of human loving is impossible without God; the more purified and authentic it is, the more completely it can be identified with divine love. 'In relationship', Stephen and Ondrea Levine teach in their new tape set, *To Love and Be Loved*, 'lies all the work that needs to be done on the spiritual path; the confrontation with our grief, fear, distrust and judgement. In the deepest spiritual practices, one discovers that pure awareness and pure love are indistinguishable.' It was, after all, in Jesus' sensitive human presence to his relationships, in his attentive struggles with them, in all his human loveableness, in his attractiveness as a deeply caring human being, that God's essence was revealed and that the church was founded. It was in the warmth of his smile, the look in his eyes, the magnetism of his awareness of people's guilt and fear, that God wished to be accessible to the world. For the Christian, there is no other way to worship the sacred, human heart of God.

Given our human condition, in time and space, and given God's assumption of that finite condition as the full and sufficient medium of continuing revelation, there is nothing any more concerning the reality of God in Jesus that lies outside of humanity, of human experience, of the totality of creation. *To simply be* is to be able, like the hub of a wheel, to hold all the vibrant spokes together. *To simply be* is to be attentive enough to the shifting surfaces of life, like a human spirit-level, bringing into right relationship what is out of true. *To simply be* is to be attuned enough to one's inner, divine harmony, so as to be a tuning fork, bringing discordant voices into true pitch. *To simply be* is to be a map, a compass, for those who are lost. The purpose of silence in our lives, of non-verbal ways of being present to ourselves and to others, is simply and precisely to heighten our awareness of the subtleties of life – those nooks and crannies in the labyrinths of our daily work and play – those nooks and crannies in which God is waiting to be found. *To simply be,* above all, is to be in our bodies. Because of God's initial desire, 'fall' or no fall, as we saw, to assume created humanity, to be transformed into flesh, God's pure being is now available in human bodies. It seems as though there is a divine obsession with the physical. From God's delight in assuming the small body of a baby, to Jesus' amazing plan to become the very flesh and bone of human beings through our eating and drinking of his own body in the medium of bread and wine, it is no wonder that, in a more enlightened orthodoxy, the body and all its spiritual and sexual powers is seen as the very tabernacle of divinity

The Santa Fe bus
I'm sitting up front. Hale, the driver, wants to talk. He's been at the wheel all day. Started out this morning in Denver. He tells me many interesting incidents from his decades of driving across the States. He's full of information. He points towards the Sandia Peak in the distant Cibola Forest, and mentions the 250 million year-old dinosaur Coelophysis whose fossils were discovered there. 'Take the cable-car up,' he helpfully suggests. (Which I did, the following day.) It is 94 degrees in the bus. The air-conditioning has failed. Someone spots a raccoon. Everyone has something to say. We see new casinos mushrooming all over the desert. Hale asks me what I do. I tell him. He himself does not practice, but his wife 'goes every day'. For a while we share in a familiar and comfortable kind of Catholic-speak.

Throughout all of this I'm very aware of the reality of what's going on. I'm trying to live in the present moment, in all of its dimensions. If the theological position I'm holding in these pages is true, then one of the most perfect ways of communion with God right now is by giving my full attention to what is happening inside the Santa Fe bus. The true contemplative lives in the present. So does the prophet and the mystic. So did Jesus. On the Sante Fe bus, I was trying not to stay on the surface of things, of our intermittent conversations, of the sensations of my senses as we looked around us and out through the windows. I was rejoicing at the way community happened so suddenly amongst us – total strangers having a laugh about a negative situation (the broken-down air-conditioning); I was reflecting on the sobering appearance of so many exploitative gambling emporiums in the high desert and, with great delight, on the glimpses, in the distance, of the hard evidence for what is now called The New Story (the tracing of our origins, our infancy, with increasing accuracy over the past 15-18 billion years since the Big Bang).

As we wondered at the geological layers and eras of the Sandia Peak granite and limestone in terms of pre-historic millennia, which they wondrously were, I was seeing them too as pages from the diaries of God and snap-shots from the albums of divine becoming. *To simply be*, in the subtitle of this piece, is, in one sense, not so simple really. *To simply be* means to be present in full depth, to be at the level of the really real, to be aware of the context of mystery in which any awareness happens, to move beyond a surface existence. *To simply be* avoids the trap of dualism. It sees Jesus as the sacrament of awareness of what was already created by his Father, and as the revealer of the love and meaning that permeates all things. The good news of salvation is not something completely new added on to, or replacing what went wrong earlier, but rather the clarification and completion, by Jesus' passover, of God's loving design to create and save the world, the initial fruit of God's womb.

The mystery-filled moment of incarnation revealed and reveals the rich levels of significance that lie beyond, behind, below and around everything that is, and that happens. Whatever we perceive with the senses is surrounded by an infinity of wonder. Since Jesus, we know that the universal being that permeates and draws all things from the beginning of time, is truly personal. And more than that, we know that this personal life-force and energy, active and at work in all things since the first creation, is not only personal, but is intimately so. When we look, from the Santa Fe bus, at those smooth and craggy rocks of ages along the summit of the Sandia Peak, we can discern, with the eyes of faith, the clever, beautiful face of a totally committed lover, whose intense gaze is directed to each one of us alone, and to all of us together. *To simply be* is to be a traveller who is learning to be familiar with the contours of this magic land called our lives, who is expectant of the surprises hidden in every new moment, who continually and delightedly explores the most ordinary of things and is never disappointed. And who also knows that the only place for all of this to happen is a little-known and mostly uninhabited countryside, quite close to all of us, called the present moment.

Sacraments of simply being

As straight as railway-lines, to the north and south of where I'm
sitting just now, the Gulf of Mexico meets the Galveston main-
land. During these last days of my sabbatical in the States, I'm
still trying to draw out and hold together the old and the new,
from the mysteries of creation and incarnation. As I watch the
regular, brown waves unfolding themselves along the empty
shore, I'm wondering about the role of the liturgy in this holy
work. On the one hand, *to simply be* before God and the world
will draw us into personal, intimate experiences of darkness and
light that belong beyond mental or verbal words or images. On
the other hand, *to simply be* before God and the world will also
draw us into the need for some kind of public, ritualistic expression or celebration of our experiences. One sentence from the
library of Karl Rahner's writings has lead me into exhilarating
ways of revisioning liturgy. Sacraments celebrate what is already there. Again, it is all about being attentive to the way
things are. Without this awareness, we are back in a dualistic
mode where the sacred and the secular belong to different
worlds.

Before liturgical celebration in church can make any Christian
sense, the liturgy of the world must first be entered into. The
Irish poet Patrick Kavanagh finds God 'in the bits and pieces' of
daily life. Rahner is convinced that 'we will be only able to
recognise the presence of the absolute mystery in the liturgy if
we first recognise its abiding presence throughout our whole
lives and in all the world'.[42] Writing about this loving mystery
that is easily ignored or overlooked because of its hidden nature,
he feels the need to 'dig it out, so to speak, from under the refuse
of the ordinary business of life'. This detection of the quiet gift of
the abundant life, waiting to be discovered in the shadow and
light of each night and day, is the work of the mystic.

I have tried, in recent articles and books, to unravel a strand
of traditional incarnational theology to underpin all that I have
written here, including the belief that we must enter into and
celebrate the liturgy of life before we can truly celebrate the
liturgy of the sacraments.[43] This, in fact, is not all that difficult to
do. Most of our best theologians, poets and mystics throughout
the centuries of Christianity are excitingly clear about a theology
of creation and about the principles of sacramentality. Once we
make the paradigm shift from a dualistic, 'redemption-only'

interpretation of incarnation, into a wider and more creation-centred understanding of salvation and revelation, then the old doctrines of our faith become pregnant with new possibilities, opening out before us like a freshly-furrowed field waiting for the new grain of our transformed consciousness.

Every time we celebrate the saving mysteries of creation and incarnation, we remember and reactivate God's initial creative work and God's subsequent and continuing redemptive action in the past and present. We affirm, celebrate and intensify the constant presence of grace in our midst from the fiery beginning of our cosmic story, through the fifteen billion years of evolution, into the current thrusting, straining and groaning of the world, forever painfully giving birth to new beauty. In his Prologue, John reminds us that Love has always been incarnate. This story of the continual unfolding of God's love for us is true of everything from the personal details of our own painful, joyful, inner and outer journeys to the stunning revelations of the mysteries of the cosmos.

Slow dawn over Lebh Shomea

Pray as you can, not as you should

It is dark night all over Texas. I'm sitting near a window in my little dwelling at Lebh Shomea House of Prayer, situated some sixty miles south of Corpus Christi. It is 5.00 am and the silence is intense. I am sitting before my God with a 'listening heart' (*lebh shomea*, 1 Kings 3:9). This, for me, is not a familiar way of praying. I usually talk and God listens. Soon the first, tentative flush of morning will reflect off the turrets of the imposing La Parra Ranch House in the distance, with its red roof-tiles and white stucco walls. The light will come slowly, first a rolling carpet of amber across the tops of the trees and then, from the low edge of the sky, the parallel streaks of pink and puce and purple will reach upwards, like a magic stairway, in pursuit of the last few fading stars. With the dawning of the new day, some of the citizens of this semi-tropical vegetation, such as the armadillos, racoons and the nilgai, will shyly fade back into the undergrowth, and the more confident ones, like the javelinas, the geckos and the road-runners will emerge. And, up in the trees, as though they cannot contain themselves for another second, the cicadas, who live for one night only, with no warning at all, will erupt in a shrill and deafening cacophany of mating calls.

It is now 6.00 am. And just as the sublime tones of the violin descend stealthily, like shy beauty, into the heart of the throbbing symphony, lifting it and transforming its loveliness, so too the pure peals of the angelus bell ring out across Lebh Shomea. They dance over the Texas daisies and the Indian paintbrush, and flow around the waving oleanders and the arthritic mesquite trees. A grazing deer just lifts its head; a wild turkey makes a small hop. Into this Eden-moment, full of wonder and innocence, the angel's song is sung again, the Word is spoken. It is the Word that reveals the love and meaning at the heart of another dawn. It is the Word that reminds us that the light of the brightening sky is revealing none other than the longing face of our divine lover. Long after they have grown silent, those bells will still make music in my heart. They are the small sacrament of the real presence of God in all that is happening. They remind me that the dance of creation and incarnation never stops, now that the night of fear is over. And so I worship the God who is at work and at play this very moment, rejoicing in the renewed being of all creatures. *Haec est dies quam fecit Dominus.* Yes. Amen. A new day has just begun.

The lifestyle of the mixed Christian community here, under the auspices of the Missionary Oblates of Mary Immaculate, is contemplative-eremitical. Lebh Shomea, during the desert experience, is a no-frills place of silence. A Centre Point in Sherwood Forest it is most certainly not! They are long, the nights of wondering, the days of waiting, the hours of praying. Apart from the occasional cool breezes that blow inland, like airy graces, from the Gulf of Mexico, it is searingly hot in the summer. Distractions are reduced to a minimum. It is amazing what we can live without – our friends, daily news, TV (including Olympic Trials, Wimbledon Tennis, the British Open Golf, the Tour de France), our favourite food and drink, talking, hugging, being important, working, playing, weekends. The Lebh Shomea desert is a relentless moment for the hidden truth about ourselves to surface to awareness, and that emergence always entails a painful and joyful season of being lost and of being found. The desert is not a dead place. Somewhere, as the Little Prince observed, it hides a well.

Noisy contemplation

I mention here but one example of the kind of transformation that can happen in a divine milieu such as Lebh Shomea. I have always struggled with prayer. I have struggled with the Divine Office, charismatic singing, many devotional and repetitive litanies, yoga, Buddhist 'sitting', Zen meditation, careful lists of petitions – universal and personal, and guided imagery. I have loved them at times, set them aside at others. Sometimes, and wisely, I have prayed as I was able to; very often I forced the river and tried to pray as I thought I was supposed to. My sojourn here at the House of Prayer is obviously a part of my spiritual journey into the world of prayer. I wasn't long here when I came across this passage in a book by Fr Kelly Nemeck, co-founder and director of Lebh Shomea: 'After a lifetime of saying prayers and of much fruitful mental activity during prayer, we discover ourselves wanting to just sit and be quiet with God. We want to listen to him, without necessarily hearing anything at all. We are content to remain silent for awhile. Indeed, we need to be quiet. This is in marked contrast to our previous habits of praying.'[44]

My previous habits of prayer leave much to be desired. I have excused myself with hit-and-miss sporadic efforts, cobbling together bits and pieces of recited prayers from liturgical and para-liturgical duties and devotions in my ministry to parishioners. This, of course, is hardly prayer at all. What is emerging and clarifying itself for me, these days, is the acute need for more structure and depth, more richness and resonance in the time I spend alone with God. Too long have I fobbed God off with excuses about my pastoral work as coming first and, after all, when I'm visiting someone in hospital am I not spending time with God? Of course I am, in one sense but, in another, not really. If these forty days in the stifling desert of Lebh Shomea have opened the eyes of my soul to anything it is to this huge empty space in my spiritual life. This reflection is about my awareness of another way of being present to God – it could be called a contemplative way of praying, yet a very 'ordinary' one.

There is no dualism in this 'ordinary' way of contemplating. We call on all of creation to facilitate our way to God's heart, to gaze on God's face. Our imagination, our internalised spirituality of the heart, our lived theology of creation, the creative arts, guided meditation, visualisation, rituals and all traditional and contemporary practices for deepening the interior life, are part of active contemplation in so far as they lead us to a still place of restful presence before God. They facilitate, on the one hand, a state of wakefulness regarding the divine milieu we inhabit, the human condition in which we find ourselves and, on the other, an awareness of the indwelling Blessed Trinity deep in our souls. They draw us through the satisfaction and pleasures of the 'natural' world, transcending them, mysterious though they are, into the finer joys of the spiritual life. They lead us towards an ultimate abandonment of our lives, our hopes, our future into the care of divine providence.

L'Adorable

When we plan to meet, there is only real contentment and intimacy between my friend and myself, when our relationship is nurtured while we are apart. If there is no mutual mindfulness or nourishing awareness between meetings, then a rare reson-

ance and intangible rapport is missing when we do encounter
each other physically. I have noticed the same principle here
also, in my current attempts to sit with the Lord for three hours
or more each day. When I'm busy about other things such as my
manual work, my spiritual reading, my journal, my cards to my
friends, my peek at yesterday's newspaper, and rush to 'squeeze
in' the allotted sessions of prayer, then the quality of my presence is clearly lacking in a certain kind of ease. But when I try to
spend all of my day – my walking or cycling, my avoidance of
the javelinos or diamondback snakes, my eating and constant re-
filling of my water-bottles, my note-taking and my writing of
this reflection – with an aware, contemplative mind rather than
with a distracted, calculating mind, then the transition into a
more focused time with God is more satisfying and wholesome.

To be able to live fully in the present moment, to be in time
and tune with God's immanence, is an extraordinary grace. To
be able to see beyond the appearances into the 'isness' of things,
to be able to perceive something of the depth of what is always
going on around us, to be able to discern the face of God, however
faintly, at the centre of what allures our senses, is the grace of the
mystic. And likewise with all that damages, hurts and diminishes
us. To be equally receptive of the divine hand in the hundred
faces of the cross as well as of the Joy, is the mark of the true contemplative. There can be no other authentic route to the heart of
God; no other way to be true to the mystery of creation and incarnation. And, since we are all well acquainted with the 'sin of
the world', that flawed strain in our human condition that seduces
us at our weakest point, this route is carved out of the wilder-
ness of many personal conversions and small deaths.

'Everything that happens is adorable.' Who else but a mystic
such as Teilhard de Chardin could sum up so much wisdom so
pithily? (The word 'adorable' here, translated from the French,
points to the indwelling sacredness of matter, and is not to be
understood in any colloquial sense.) It takes immense innocence
of vision and surrender of will to perceive true divinity in all
that goes on. '. . . something is truly adorable,' writes Fr Nemeck,
'only when we have done our maximum to bestow on creatures
the utmost reality that Christ desires us to give them and when
we have left ourselves receptive to the optimum spiritual energy
which they have to endow us . . . To experience l'*Adorable* in
everything that happens is unquestionably a receptivity of a

superior order. This is especially true when it is a question of the cross and of detachment . . .'[45]

This way of praying is like placing a transforming filter between our eyes and what we see, so that everything is perceived in the light of the death and resurrection of Jesus. It is like what happens when the small, indecipherable slide (of our ambiguous experiences) is expanded into its true colours on the screen (of our consciousness) by the light (of revelation) of the projector. What is so exciting about this kind of intimacy with God, each moment of our days and nights, is that it is achieved, not by short-circuiting, denying, ignoring or down-grading any sensate, sensible or sensual human experience, but by being fully present to them. To truly love someone else, for example, is already to be living in and loving God, and to be experiencing, to some extent, the cauterising wound of divine passion.

In so far as contemplative prayer is a temporary ceasing from our external activity, work and various ministries, this ceasing is only to equip us all the better to return to them with mind, heart and body renewed. We ponder in silence, in the sands of the spirit, only so as to be all the more sure of the way we walk on the streets of life when we return. We enter into to the solitude of the mountains from our travels in the busy valley, so as to see more clearly and with perspective, the hidden hazards and potential wrong turnings of those travels. Jesus took his disciples aside to a quiet place, on occasion, so as to purify and intensify the spirit that animated their intense apostolate. This is to be true to a theology of creation which holds that it is only when we fully enter into the reality of life, when we immerse ourselves totally in our humanity, when we go all the way through the createdness of our condition, bringing all that we encounter with us, that we can finally approach the heart of God. We respect, honour and adore the creation of God even as we love and worship the God of creation. It is as though we penetrate into the heart of nature, assuming it in its entirety, as God did in the initial creation and as Jesus did, later in time but first in the primordial divine intention. And then, dressed in the garb of the world, and in our complete and fully entered-into humanity, we respond to God's call to the intimacy of God's incarnate heart and home. If, then, we make this contemplative habit of mind and heart like second nature to us, the time we spend alone with God in personal prayer will be rich and transforming.

Come as you are
When, for instance, you open your door to the passing traveller, what you see before you is the person who has lived through every minute of the decades of their years, who have passed through their lives' experiences, dealing with them the best way they could, enduring the deserts of their destiny and enjoying the pastures of their pleasures too. In essence, you see that person and no other. Nor can it be otherwise. Likewise with us before God. We are there, in contemplation, as the sum of our experiences, at our highest and at our lowest, in our graces and in our sins, in all that makes for growth and all that brings diminishment. To approach God in any other pretext or disguise, to attempt to reach that heart through any other door, is to get hopelessly lost in the darkness of dualism. It is to deny everything that has been revealed by our compassionate Lover in the most touching and beautiful mystery of the incarnation. Why do we find it so difficult to believe in our own beauty?

> Do you know how beautiful you are?
> I think not, my dear.
> For as you talk of God,
> I see great parades with wildly marching bands
> Streaming from your mind and heart,
> Carrying wonderful and secret messages
> To every corner of the world.
>
> I see saints bowing in the mountains
> Hundreds of miles away
> To the wonder of sounds
> That break into light
> From your most common words.
>
> . . . Do you know how beautiful you are?
>
> I think not, my dear.
>
> Yet Hafiz
> Could set you upon a Stage
> And worship you forever![46]

Nevertheless, as a wary and awkward newcomer to the practice of a more silent and solitary kind of contemplation, though still based completely, as above, on the mystery of the Word-made-Flesh, I find it an unfamiliar place to be. It lies beyond the threshold of the way I normally pray. It brings the reality of my loving relationship with God on to another plane. It exposes it to another light. Even an introduction to contemplation calls for profound trust, relentless letting go and a graced capacity for living in the present moment. It has much to do with waiting, yet not knowing that for which we are waiting. I had not realised how important my plans and agendas were to me, how strong my control needs were, how significant in my life was the issue of power, how urgent, intense and impatient the tempo of my days had become. A commitment to contemplative prayer presumes an acceptance of powerlessness, a surrender to another, a settling for not knowing. My courage and faith are stretched to the limits. This indeed is a kind of dying; because there is no certainty, no way to 'fix it', no method, path or formula. With blunt, precise and almost shocking words, St John of the Cross puts it this way:

In order to experience pleasure in all *(todo)*,
Desire to have pleasure in nothing *(nada)*.
In order to arrive at possessing all,
Desire to possess nothing.
In order to arrive at being all,
Desire to be nothing.
In order to arrive at knowing all
Desire to know nothing. (*The Ascent of Mount Carmel* 1, 13, 11.)

First faltering steps
So here I am, like the boy I once was, turning up for school on that first day, my copybook and pencil in my new leather bag. There is so much to learn. The world of contemplation is such a special, elusive place. Yes, here I am; show me! After all, there was a day when someone said to a young Shakespeare, 'This is how you form an A, a B, a C' and someone once said to a (very) young Beethoven, 'That sound is a do, a re, a me'. But then, it's probably not like that at all. No one actually teaches contemplative prayer. Who teaches the wind to blow, the baby to smile, the river to flow? Who teaches our hearts to love? Maybe there is no laboured learning, no didactic teaching; more like an unlearning, a wisdom that emerges by subtraction. Maybe the student waits for the midwife to come and draw forth the mystery already safely held within.

The way of contemplation, while challenging and strange to our urgent, stimulation-seeking minds, is, in a sense, a natural grace of the heart. Given half a chance, the contemplative dim-

ension within us, especially within children, will come out to
play. Recent European research testifies overwhelmingly to this
(but not in a formal religious sense). Our restless hearts are always yearning for something just beyond. Deep calls to deep,
mystery responds to mystery. Like a small child before a steep
fairground slide, we are filled with both fear and fascination. We
hesitate. We are risking the unknown abyss when we trustingly
lay our heads, as the beloved disciple did, on the breast of Jesus.
This is a threshold moment. It is as though all that has happened
in our lives, previously, has prepared us for some kind of radical
breakthrough now. There is a transformation of consciousness
about to happen. We feel some kind of inevitability about it.
And there will be no going back. From some journeys we cannot
return. There are fleeting glimpses that we cannot forget. The
possibility of resting in God alone is one of these.

The contemplative way is not a way at all. So we must get off
the one we're on! The secret is that there is no secret. Our underlying desire is, in fact, to have no desire. The content we seek is
emptiness. The place we're going to is nowhere. There is no
project or process that can access this inner state of soul. To be
still enough to hear the heartbeat of God in everything does not
come through our effort alone. The ability to 'remain loving the
Beloved' is the work of God. We call it grace. It is pure gift. And
it is offered to all. We then become free with a freedom we never
tasted before – a primal kind of freedom to be our true self, to inhabit our soul, to live out of our own truth no matter what. That
is what contemplation offers us – the freedom to simply be.

Something tells me that the most difficult, confusing, deeply
uprooting and exciting stretches of my spiritual journey up to
now are only beginning. And there seems to be very few sign-
posts or 'you are here' charts along the way. It is unfamiliar territory where values and virtues are radically altered. The terrifying
demons that spring up, as if from nowhere, shake us to the core
of our being. How will I ever negotiate the paradoxes, seduc-
tions and contradictions of this desert-journey – the oases and
the mirages, the blinding sand-storms and the equally blinding
white light? But if we hang on by the finger-tips of our faith and
with all the help we can find (especially by way of a spiritual
director) then the rumour of angels becomes a reality. We will
find the inner courage to continue with the adventure, with all
its dread, excitement and discovery. The Muslim mystic Shams-
ud-din Mohammed Hafiz wrote,

Pulling out the chair
Beneath your mind
And watching you fall upon God –
There is nothing else for Hafiz to do
That is any fun in this world![47]

'Ah, ah Lord; I am only a child'
It is one thing to be with someone each day, talking, playing, doing things. Plans are worked out together, stories are shared, promises are made. It is quite another thing to sit in silence with that person, to savour the flavour of their presence, to be fully at ease in that experience of awareness, to wish for nothing else but the peaceful intensity and relaxed attention of that moment. In spite, of course, of many differences, contemplation, to my mind, is something like that. It requires a certain kind of discipline for such non-focused listening and self-forgetfulness to become a habit of the heart. Without the gift of love and trust, or at least the true desire to be filled with those twin blessings of nature and grace (in so far as grace and nature can ever be separated) I doubt if contemplative prayer could ever be sustained. What follows are some novice-notes I am making (they may seem childish and over-simple) about my initial focus or springboard, as I begin each hour of being simply present and attentive, in inner wordless and imageless silence, before the Love that is deep within me and all around me.

The house
I come before you again today, O God of the Morning, O Sheltering God, with the words of St Paul to the Ephesians still in my heart. You are the 'cornerstone' of my house, of my spiritual journey. Everything must be 'aligned' on you. You are the spirit-level, the plumb-line, the set-square that puts me in 'right relation' with my sisters and brothers, the flora and the fauna, the four elements, the four directions, the earth itself and the universe it inhabits. You are not just another room in the building of my soul. You are the whole fabric, its atmosphere and its essence. Nor is anything else shut out by its doors and walls. I am a child of the universe and carry all of evolution within me. This dwelling of the Trinity houses the world. All of creation inhabits this house. That is why, since the Word became flesh, it is the real presence of God, the blessed sacrament of God's intimacy.

Only the house of matter can be the house of spirit. All I ask of you, O Gracious Host, is to let me spend some time silently with you now, to contemplate this mystery, to be here as your unprofitable but profoundly precious servant; to do nothing but remain loving you, my Beloved; to dwell in the house of my Lord forever. (Ps 23:6)

The baby

Like the small, sleeping baby spread across the body of its mother, I too fall into you, my Mother God. The baby, fruit of the love of its parents, needs nothing new but nourishment and love to grow into its fullness. Nurtured in loving arms it grows as a tree grows, expanding from its centre; it unfolds as a flower does, becoming what it already is. At my centre, too, O God, is your very life. Your seed is within me; it will blossom into you. All I do is let myself be loved by you. I am already, in my essence, everything you desire me to be. In peace, without expectation, I simply stay looking at your divine face. I remain loving you, my beloved. I rest in your arms. Free from anxiety, and in no hurry, I am open only to your will for me. I rely on nothing, anymore, but you. I am empty of everything except my desire for you and the responsibilities of the present moment. I am content, this evening, my daily tasks over, to behold you, to gaze at you, and to wait in repose, in trust and in wonder. And in the waiting, my desire for you will be purified and intensified so that both our desires will become one.

The sponge

Like the dry sponge that falls into the ocean, I too immerse myself silently in you, my God of abundance. I let the transformation happen to me. You ask for nothing from me only to let myself be filled with you. I swing and sway and flow on the waves of your supporting richness. You hold me in your great mercy; you embrace me with unutterable tenderness. I have no fear. Your overwhelming delight in me has taken it all away. I am happy just to be. I no longer try to make headway, force myself to be better, striving to please you and to win your graces. All of my striving, in fact, only prevented you from blessing me with the very beauty I longed for. I now surrender to your rhythm and timing. I hand my soul itself, without anxiety, over to you. And in the giving over of my life to you, my heart will be

washed into its true colours, and my soul burnished to reflect
your gold. Only close to the cross does this purifying take place.
But then, O Wounded Healer, in the desert, you and the cross
throw the same shadow. This morning, I place no more obstacles
in your path. For the next hour and always, I am yours to do
with me as you want to. Here I am, Lord, just me before you.

The child

A little boy goes out walking, holding his father's hand. He is
confident and secure; he is brave and smiling. Through the
touch of his father, he can feel the strength flow into his own
body and heart. O God, you are my father; I am the little boy.
You are holding my hand. And that is everything. Your power is
mine; I become more aware of your vision. I am flesh of your
flesh, bone of your bone. As the acorn seed becomes the oak,
with nothing added but time, so do I grow more closely into
you. I do not have to try. You long to pour your precious and
lovely treasures into my life. All I have to do is to keep holding
your hand, to keep looking at your face. All that I searched so
desperately for, all that I urgently achieved and clung to, all that,
with intense effort, I tried to master, have lost their attraction for
me. It is you alone who now fills my heart, mind and body. All I
have to do is to get out of my own way and let you be you. 'It is
enough to simply be,' I hear you say, 'You are home, at last.' For
this hour today, we are each other's gracious guests as we honour each other in silence. May it remain this way all my life.

The seed

Like a seed in the earth, I curl up in you, O God. And like the
seed that has to do nothing to grow, as the sun, the soil, the rain
draw out from within its essence what is already there, so too
with me, O divine Mother. Created in your image, there is no
more to add on. By surrendering to your light, warmth and nurturing moisture, the healing and wholeness will happen – is
happening. I am content to wait until, according to your will and
wisdom, the season for pruning and blossoming comes along.
Without a worry about the details of my worthiness, I let go of
all thoughts and emotions of guilt, doubt and sinfulness. I only
know that you love me more than I could ever imagine; that all
you want is for me to let you love me. There is nothing I can do
to make you love me one bit more or less. My heart is overflow-

ing with gratitude. That is enough for now. From this moment, and in silence, I let your tender, abundant mother's love wash over and through every self-caused rockfall of sin that blocks my journey to you. During this hour, whether I know it or not, you are preparing the way, making ready the path, where we will walk and talk forever.

The water-drop

You are the ocean, my God and I am the fish. You surround me, you fill me, you sustain me; you are before me, behind me, below me, above me. In you I live and move and have my being. I cannot escape from you even if I wanted to. And to do so would be death. I swim in your very being. You are the grace and energy in everything I do, think, say and feel. I am the drop of water that disappears into your river. I lose my ego, my false self and find my true identity in you. I must decrease and you must increase. This decreasing may mean my readiness to be flung into torrents and over waterfalls in blind leaps of trust. In this death to myself, O Tremendous Lover, I become more radiantly human and truly free than ever before. So now, I let myself fall into you and sink into your heart. I make no other effort. I allow myself to be transformed into you, however and whenever you chose. This morning, I am content to sit here and wait. I am happy just to be here, a fish in your ocean, a water-drop in your river.

The moment

I give myself over to the present moment. You live nowhere else, O God of the Now. I look no further for the guidance that I need. Only here am I safe with you. I leave aside all my plotting and planning to be better tomorrow, to improve with time, to merit your compassion by pleasing you more. I am receptive to whatever is calling me in the here and now. This is your authentic voice, telling me all I need to know; your angel guarding me every moment, even in the valley of death. I am no longer afraid because it is you who walk with me. That is why I want to rest now, in the present, liberated from the whining echoes of the past and the anxious warnings about the future. I give myself over to this moment. It is the only place I can be at home with you; the only space that is safe. It is the one doorway to each other's heart, the one room for our intimacy to be deepened.

And so, this evening, I wait without inner or outer words, in this place, attentive to your loveliness, in peace, in readiness, in hope.

The mystery

Your mystery is in me from the beginning, O Lord of all. Your being is my being. That means that I carry within me your creativity, your artistry, your beauty, your healing, your imagination, your redemptive power. All I need to do is become aware of their presence in my soul. By virtue of your self-gift at my birth and of Jesus' self-gift at my baptism, the new life is breaking through each day. I simply claim it with a full heart. O Loving Lord, O Mystery of my life, just to be is blessed and to live is holy because you are being and life, abundant and mysterious. Unbidden, you are all around us, you flow through us; all we have to do is to go with that flow. Nothing more is required; the river of life knows well how to take care of us. I abandon myself to your divine providence. With your grace, I surrender completely to the mystery that you are. I will now sit in silence before you, without prayers, without images, and let my whole life fall into your holy hands.

The gaze

This hour, O my Saving God, is to behold you, to gaze at you, just to be near you. Today I bring no requests or prayers of any kind except to be blessed by your presence as I adore you. No more will I ask for things, even for the holiest favours. It is enough to be here – more than enough. I don't know any more how to overcome distractions, resist temptations, avoid sinning. Nor do I know which is the swiftest path to you. From now on it does not matter. My knowledge is misleading. My petitions are unnecessary. If I'm lost in the desert, then so be it. If I'm hot and tired and in a dry place, I continue to trust. You have the calendar, you have the watch, you have the map and you have the overall plan. From now on, may I be drawn by you, not self-driven; beckoned onwards by you, not self-motivated. I am so weary of striving. I believe that you love me. While I wait for what I do not know, I know that it is you who are waiting in me. And now, for this hour, this morning, while I wait, I will gaze on your face.

The breath

As I sit in hope, without expectation, O Breath of my life, I listen to my own breath. As I sit with you, awake and aware, I feel you in my inhaling and exhaling. O God of life, O Beat of my heart, you fill my body and soul with your presence. I look for you nowhere else. O Pure Being, O Source of Creation, you are the very loving energy that keeps my lungs and my heart opening and closing, gifting me, unfailingly, with miraculous life as you first did with Adam at the beginning. When I am close to my breath I am close to you. You are my most intimate part. My breathing leads me to you. All is contained in your Divine Breath, like the day in the morning's dawn. We come into this world on the breath of your compassion, and we go out of this world on the breath of your mercy. Through breathing I descend, wordlessly, into the abyss within myself, where you live. It is there that we become inseparable. It is in my very stillness that you are vibrant. And so I am filled with love as, for the next hour, I simply breathe.

The word

Just the one word I listen for, O God of Wisdom, the one word so I know you're there for me – to reassure my frightened and confused heart. Yet the silence is enough. You teach me to live with the silence, with the emptiness, with the *nada*. I don't do it very well. It can't be much pleasure for you to see me so distracted, tired or tuned out. But is the mother turned off when her baby sleeps or cries? I try to keep my mind quiet so that your word may be written on it. I try to still the noise to hear your whisper. Maybe tomorrow; maybe next year; maybe never. With a wild patience, I wait. But you have spoken your Word. At Mass today, in raw bread and red wine, that Word has now become the very fibre of my body, flesh of my flesh and bone of my bone. We are no longer distinguishable. Not only have I heard your Word, I am your Word. To be aware of myself is to be aware of you. St Augustine prayed, *noverim me ut noverim te*. To live in my body, to feel my soul, is to live and experience you. In this faith I simply put my arm around you and lean against you.

The touch

Under your healing touch, O Divine Physician, I sleep. I do not stop your hand anymore. You are the one who restores my soul to health. I have tried too often to heal myself and failed. I am weary of striving. I cannot set myself free. The blockages are too many. Under the anaesthetic of your holy power, I believe and wait. One day you will unblock all my resistances to your life-giving energy – my physical, emotional, spiritual and mental blockages. Each day the awareness of my sickness, weakness, addictions and negative compulsions grow stronger. I am powerless before them, twisting and turning as I do, to shake off their grip on my soul. I do so no longer. I finally trust and submit to your infinite commitment my total well-being. My life is in your hands. It is not in mine anymore. I await your touch of fire, your wound of love. As I fall more in love with you, the chains that bind me now will fall away without effort. In the silence of my waiting I praise you and I thank you with each breath I draw, with each beat of my heart.

The well

My well was dry until you came. It was blocked with buried debris. I was trying to fill it from the top. Worn out with fruitless effort, I had to hand it over to you. Now with the first springing into new life of the long-repressed water much is happening. While a peace and satisfaction renew my life, I'm also more aware of so much rubbish now floating on the new water – all the forces that have damaged and diminished my true self. In a flash I see my sins, the pain of those I've hurt, the lost opportunities, the foolish, unnecessary mistakes. I'm learning not to panic at this unpleasant sight. 'This is the hour,' writes Teilhard de Chardin, 'of the specifically Christian operation when Christ, preserving in us all the treasures of our nature, empties us of our egocentrism and takes our heart. . . (But) it is a salvific hour for the person enlightened by faith who experiences him/herself being liberated from selfishness and dying by the force of a communion.'[48] There is no fear in me now as, after another hard day, I prepare to rest my head, without explanation or self-consciousness, on my Beloved. The constant, easy pushing of the sweet, spring water is effortlessly doing its work in the landscape of my soul.

The heart

O Sacred, Human Heart of God, *Gile mo chroí*, I place all my trust in you. Yours is the heart that beats in the tiniest insect and in the mightiest galaxy. Yours is the heart that inspires the hope in the most hopeless of us, the vision in those who are building cities in space. Next to you, tonight, O Hero of my heart, I lay down my own heart. What a privilege to listen to the rhythm of that infinite pulse that first sounded, for us at least, in the big creative bang fifteen billion years ago, that throbs with pure energy in everything now that lives, and that reaches its perfect pitch and point in the loving human heart! All I feel just now, my dearest Heart, is an overwhelming sense of humility, gratitude and deepest wonder. To think that I will now be in your vibrant presence for a silent hour, to know that you love my company and are delighted to be with me, that all I need to do is let you love me. Give me, your servant, O Lover of my life, a listening heart – *lebh shomea.*

Glossary

Process: An organic way of developing and growing in aware-ness of our body-mind-spirit unity. It is not product-oriented. It is more about the way of doing rather than about what is done. In the context of this book, 'process' signifies a holistic approach to the inner work of the soul. All of the following approaches, exercises and practices are examples of 'process' work.

Bodywork: Any work that enhances body-awareness. It 'fleshes out' into our physical dimension what we carry in our heads. This process includes all forms of massage, breathing tech-niques, dance and movement, certain kinds of exercise, art as therapy and rituals.

Holotropic Practice: Holotropic means 'moving towards whole-ness'. Holotropic Breathwork, pioneered by Dr Stanislav Grof, is a technique for gaining access to a non-ordinary state of consciousness through deep, fast breathing. The healing is facilitated by evocative music.

Reiki: This is a pure energy form rediscovered by Dr Mikao Usui in Japan, in the mid-nineteenth century. Reiki is a healing practice where the universal life-force energy flows through the attuned Master into the body, mind and spirit of the receiver, through the placing of hands.

Enneagram: This ancient tool for spiritual growth belongs to an Eastern tradition of Sufi wisdom. Oscar Ichazo is credited with bringing it to public attention, first in Chile and then in the USA. Centred around nine personality types, it has to do with becoming aware of the shadows, 'sins' and compulsions that make us who we are.

Parental Process: An intensive programme, associated with Robert Hoffman (USA), that seeks to heal the pain of child-hood, and transform the negative and self-defeating habits that so commonly dominate people's lives.

T'ai Chi Chih: These twenty joyous, meditative movements, orig-inated by Justin Stone, a teacher of Eastern disciplines, circulate the vital energy, renewing and balancing the inner strength of each individual.

Feldenkrais: The Feldenkrais Method, named after the Israeli scientist Moshe Feldenkrais, is an educational system which uses movement to bring about improved functioning – in posture and breathing, in reducing stress and tension, pain and stiffness, and in developing efficient and flexible movement.

Yoga: A system of meditation and discipline widely practiced within Hinduism. It combines physical awareness and a sense of soul through appropriate bodily posture and practiced breathing.

Somatics: The study of the body. It has to do with everything we can know about how the body moves, feels, learns, remembers, heals, senses and adapts to various environments. The somatologist teaches and practices ways of reaching the wisdom and freedom already within our bodies.

Chakras: In Oriental teaching, these are seven centres of physical, spiritual and emotional energy situated within the body, moving from the root *chakra* (at the bottom of the spine – the seat of individual and tribal survival) to the crown *chakra* (at the top of the head – the seat of union with God).

Nilgai: lit. blue cow. Imported from India, where they are referred to as antelopes, into Southern Texas in 1930.

Armadillo: Burrowing, nocturnal mammal encased in an armour of small plates.

Indian paintbrush: Also known as 'the painted cup'; a bright scarlet plant of the figworth family that grows abundantly in the eastern and southern States.

Javelina: Small, black pig-like animal that runs in packs. Produces a distinctive, unpleasant odour even when not frightened.

Notes

1. Sebastian Moore, *The Furrow,* April 2000.
2. Kabir Edmund Helminski, *Living Presence,* Jeremy Tarcher/Putnam 1992, pp 53, 56.
3. Joyce Rupp, *May I have this Dance?,* Ave Maria Press 1992, p. 117
4. Mary Oliver, *Dream Work,* The Atlantic Monthly Press 1986, pp 38, 39.
5. Inspired by 'The Mirror and the Window' in *Passion for the Possible* by Daniel O'Leary, Columba Press, 1998, pp 247 seq.
6. John Kabat-Zinn, *Mindfulness Meditation,* Piatkus 1994, p xviii.
7. Nisargadatta Maharay, *I Am That,* The Acorn Press 1992 ,p 10.
8. Sogyal Rinpoche, *The Tibetan Book of Living and Dying,* Harper San Francisco 1992, p 117.
9. ibid, p 120.
10. R. S. Thomas, *R. S. Thomas: Collected Poems 1945-1990,* Phoenix Giants 1993 ,p 220.
11 Alexander Solzhenitsyn, *The Gulag Archipelago,* quoted in Connie Zweig and Jeremiah Abrams (eds), *Meeting the Shadow,* Jeremy P Tarcher 1991, Frontispiece.
12 H. H. Dalai Lama and H. C. Cutler, *The Art of Happiness,* Hodder and Stoughton 1998, p 191.
13. Richard Rohr, 'Christianity and Creation' in Albert LaChance and John E. Carroll (eds), *Embracing Earth: Catholic Approaches to Ecology,* Orbis Books 1994, p 139.
14. Sheila Cassidy, *Sharing the Darkness,* Darton, Longman and Todd 1988, p 99.
15. H. F. Vetter (ed), *The Heart of God: Prayers of Rabindranath Tagore,* Charles E. Tuttle Co Inc 1997, p 87.
16. J. M. Brinnin (ed), *A Casebook on Dylan Thomas,* quoted in Daniel O'Leary, *Windows of Wonder,* Columba Press 1991, p 14.
17. H. F. Vetter, op cit, p 55.
18. ibid, p 45.
19. Daniel O'Leary, *Lost Soul? The Catholic Church Today,* Columba Press 1999.
20. H. F. Vetter, op cit, p 46.
21. Peter de Coppens, *Divine Light and Fire,* Element 1992, p 58.
22. Richard Rohr, *Radical Grace,* Vol 13, No 2, April 2000.
23. ibid.
24. H. F. Vetter, op cit, p 50.
25. John Bate, *Damaged Beauty needs a New Design,* The Gamecock Press 1981, p 8.

26, Kabir Edmund Helminski, op cit, p 136.

27. ibid, p 139.

28. Peter de Coppens, op cit, p 59.

29. Antony de Mello, *One Minute Wisdom*, Doubleday 1985, p 27.

30. Joan Chittister in *Spirituality*, Sept/Oct 1999.

31. ibid.

32. R. S. Thomas, op cit, p 302.

33. Karl Rahner, *Theological Investigations*, Vol XVIII, Darton, Longman and Todd 1971, p 35.

34. Gerald Vann, *The Divine Pity*, Collins 1945, p 47.

35. Peter de Coppens, op cit, p 113.

36. Mary Oliver, op cit, pp 38, 39.

37. Teilhard de Chardin, *Le Milieu Divin*, Collins 1960, p 59.

38. Mary Oliver, *Wild Geese*, op cit, p 14.

39. Thomas Menamparampil, *A Path to Prayer*, St Pauls, Bombay 1992, p 50.

40. Anthony de Mello, op cit, p 12.

41 Daniel Ladinsky, *I Heard God Laughing: Renderings of Hafiz*, Sufism Reoriented Press 1996, p 85.

42. For an excellent introduction to Karl Rahner's thoughts on these issues, see Michael Skelley, *The Liturgy of the World: Karl Rahner's Theology of Worship*, A Pueblo Book: The Liturgical Press 1991.

43. eg, Daniel O'Leary, *Passion for the Possible*, Columba Press 1998.

44. Francis Kelly Nemeck OMI and Marie Theresa Coombs, Hermit, *The Spiritual Journey*, Liturgical Press 1988, p 105.

45. Francis Kelly Nemeck OMI and Marie Theresa Coombs, Hermit, *O Blessed Night*, Alba House 1991, pp 164 & 165.

46. Daniel Ladinsky, op cit, p 33.

47. ibid, p 109.

48. Quoted in Nemeck and Coombs, *The Spiritual Journey*, op cit, pp 101 & 102.